Women Under Pressure

A Practical Guide for Today's Woman

Ursula Markham is a practising hypnotherapist dealing with every aspect of stress control in men, women, and children. She regularly addresses women's groups and organisations on the subject of pressure, as well as counselling individual patients.

Women Under Pressure

A Practical Guide for Today's Woman

Ursula Markham

ELEMENT BOOKS

© Ursula Markham 1990

First published in Great Britain in 1990 by
Element Books Limited
Longmead, Shaftesbury, Dorset

Designed by Jenny Liddle
Typeset by Selectmove
Printed and bound in Great Britain
by Richard Clay Ltd, Bungay, Suffolk
Cover design by Max Fairbrother
Cover illustration by Jennie Smith

British Library Cataloguing in Publication Data
Markham, Ursula
Women under pressure: a practical guide for today's
woman.
1. Women. Stress
I. Title
155.9042082

ISBN 1-85230-138-4

To Philip and David
with my love

'God made the country and man made the town
– And woman made Society.'

(Revd E. E. Bradford, 1860–1944)

Contents

Introduction

Why should there be a need for a book about stress in women as opposed to stress in every member of society? I can almost hear the screams of protest from the more militant members of the feminist movement who feel that I am claiming that women are different to men. Well, I am and that is the whole point – women *are* different. Not better, not worse, but definitely different. And it is this very difference which makes them vulnerable not only to all the pressures felt by men but to a whole lot more besides.

In my work as a hypnotherapist and stress management consultant I see many women, from all walks of life, who have found themselves unable to cope with the pressures forced upon them by society and, just as often, the mental, physical and emotional demands they have placed upon themselves. By the time they come to consult me professionally such women are already suffering from the effects of stress. Perhaps they are not sleeping, are suffering from migraine or problems have arisen in their relationships. Perhaps they find that they are unable to cope with life without the artificial support given by alcohol or tranquillizers on which they have come to rely. Although hope is not lost in such cases and each problem can be dealt with and overcome, how much better it would be if the situation never arose in the first place.

There you have the reason for this book. In very many cases such stress-induced problems need never arise. But to prevent them we need to look at ourselves and our lifestyle and decide what form of preventative action is appropriate. What is even more important, we need to do something which many women find exceedingly difficult – to take the time to think about ourselves. Go on, make yourself stop and think – I promise you, the results will be well worth the effort.

1

I'm Not Stressed – Or Am I?

The trouble with stress-induced problems is that they sneak up on us when we are not looking. Now, if stress were a great big sledge-hammer which delivered such a tremendous blow that there could be no mistaking its presence, things would really be much simpler. After all, if Mary Smith has her leg in a plaster cast after an accident, she would not dream of 'dashing down to the shops', would she? She would be happy to sit with her leg resting on a footstool, receiving and accepting the sympathetic noises of well-intentioned friends. But let Mary Smith be suffering from a build-up of stress in her life and not only are there no friends around to make sympathetic noises (probably because our Mary puts on such a great act that no one realises that she is in need of sympathy) but she would be unlikely to accept such expressions of concern if they did. She is far more likely to tell herself that there is no particular significance in the fact that she is smoking far more than she used to, that her periods have become rather erratic or that her children are complaining that she is growing more and more short tempered with each day that passes. She is convinced that feeling sorry for herself will not do any good at all and so she might just as well snap out of it and get on with the million and one things which need doing.

This, of course, is just the sort of attitude which is going to turn a minor stress-related problem into a major one. And when I say 'major' I really mean it. You may be able to cope with the headaches or the heavy periods but remember that it has now been proved that excessive build-up of stress can lead to such problems as strokes, cancer and heart attacks.

Stress is liberal in its choice of victims. It does not care about differences in age, class or financial status. It is just as likely to affect the young mother struggling to bring up three boisterous children on a limited income as the successful businesswoman trying vainly to juggle the varying demands of home and career. It takes its toll on the hospital cleaner just as much as on the famous television star.

But stress does not have to be the victor. You can arm yourself against it and ensure that it does not cause you any real harm at all. In this, as in many other cases, prevention is much simpler than cure. But most vital of all is self knowledge and recognition of when and how stress is beginning to have an adverse effect upon you.

First of all you need to know what stress is – and more importantly what it is *not*. It does not always have to be the villain of the piece – indeed without any stress at all our lives would be lived on a dull and monotonous plain. We all need to be able to react quickly and efficiently in a stressful situation. The mother who pulls her toddler out of the way of an approaching cyclist; the businesswoman whose quick thinking lands her company that long sought after contract; the understudy, amateur or professional, who hears that the leading lady is unable to perform that night. All these women are faced by a potentially stressful situation to which they have to respond – and respond well.

FIGHT OR FLIGHT?

What happens to you physically when you are faced with a stressful situation? You may have heard of the 'fight or flight' state – based upon the time when early man, faced with a ferocious beast had to make a split second choice between fighting the animal (perhaps to feed and clothe his family) and running for his life. To enable him not only to make the decision but to translate his thoughts into action – and to do so quickly – certain physical changes would take place in the body of our caveman hero. As adrenalin begins to flow there is an increase in the heart and pulse rate and blood pressure starts to rise. Extra blood sugar is released into the bloodstream, the muscles tense and breathing becomes more rapid. All this was designed to give him the added speed of thought and action to enable him to fight or flee.

It may be that you are unlikely to come face to face with a wild animal in your daily life but every time you find yourself in a stressful situation precisely the same physical changes take place in your body. If, like the caveman, you are then able to leap into action you will release all that energy and will do yourself no harm whatsoever. So the mother who pulls her young child out of danger will have found a use for the accumulated stress-induced energy and will suffer no ill effects. But suppose your stress is caused because you have an employer who expects miracles from you between 9am and 5pm, what can you do? Neither fight nor flight is a sensible option if you wish to keep your job. So you grit your teeth and get on with the task in hand. But what happens to the adrenalin, the tensed muscles and the increased blood pressure? They remain with you and part of you perhaps for the whole of the day. If you know nothing about dealing with a build-up of stress – or if you do not even know how to recognise that you *are* stressed – those physical effects will be with you all the way home so that you are ready to explode with anger or burst into tears as soon as someone speaks to you. And then, being a woman, you will probably feel guilty, which in turn will cause even more stress.

Now we would have to live in an ideal world indeed if we were never to come across any situations which were unfair, threatening or distressing – and this is not an ideal world. So we have to learn to deal with stressful situations while not allowing them to wreak havoc with our minds, our emotions and our bodies. At the end of this book you will find a section telling you how you can establish a simple routine which will make you far less susceptible to stress when it does arise and will help you to minimise its effects. First, however, you need to be able to recognise signs of stress in yourself so that you are able to stop and do something about it before it affects you and everyone around you.

STRESS CHECK

Look at the list of symptoms of stress which follows and see whether any of them apply to you – particularly if any of them have become more noticeable lately. If you feel that you suffer greatly from one or more of the symptoms, it would not be a bad idea to have a medical check up just to put your mind at rest. However, if no physical cause can be found for the symptoms, you can be almost certain that they are stress induced.

Headaches or migraine

There are many reasons why any of us can suffer from the occasional headache. Perhaps we have had too many late nights; we might have been sitting in the sun for longer than we should; or maybe we had a little too much to drink at that party last night. This sort of headache should not give rise to any real concern – it can happen to anyone. But if you find that your head often throbs more and more as the day progresses or if you frequently wake up with a headache then you need to look into the reasons. Perhaps the most sensible place to start is to have a check up, including having your eyes tested but if, as is often the case, the results of all tests are clear then it is quite likely that stress is to blame.

Migraine can vary greatly from one sufferer to another. While one person is plagued by a severe headache or spots before the eyes another will be unable to face daylight at all and will be overwhelmed by feelings of nausea if she even tries to sit up in bed. In many cases migraine is caused by an allergy, most commonly to alcohol, chocolate or cheese. If you know that such an allergy is the cause of your migraine then the cure is in your own hands! In the vast majority of instances, however, migraine is the direct result of excessive stress or tension and as such can be dealt with very effectively indeed. Hypnotherapy or acupuncture can provide quite remarkable cures for the symptoms of migraine but unless you do something about the cause by changing your life and refusing to allow stress to play a major role, the problem is likely to recur.

Feeling 'out of breath'

If you find that you often feel breathless or suffer from 'palpitations' without there being any obvious cause then it is quite likely that you are suffering from stress. Another symptom is hyperventilation when your breathing becomes more and more rapid and you are unable to do anything to slow it down. If, when you sit quietly or lie in bed at night, your heart seems to beat faster and faster until it sounds like a pounding in your ears, this too is often a symptom of excessive stress.

Insomnia

If your body has spent the entire day reacting to situations around you by preparing to 'fight or flee', and yet neither choice has been available to you, is it any wonder that you find it difficult to sleep? All this extra energy and adrenalin have been created – and yet they have nowhere to go. Then, of course, you become part of a vicious circle; you grow so angry and frustrated with yourself because you are unable to get to sleep that you become even more stressed, and therefore even less likely to be able to sleep.

Broken sleep and nightmares

Do you find that you are unable to sleep for more than a couple of hours at a time? If so, or if your dreams are strange and disturbing (particularly if they seem to be based upon distortions of present situations in your life), then stress is likely to be the cause. Everyone has some sort of worry or concern in their life at any time but night-time torments are unlikely to help you come up with solutions to those problems which are capable of being solved and they will certainly make you less able to cope with those which are not. You can do nothing about what has passed and you are unlikely to be able to do anything about what is to come during the night so the wisest solution is to try and find some means of relaxing before you go to bed and allow your mind and body to get the rest they require.

Nausea or vomiting

If you suffer regularly from feelings of nausea or from vomiting then the first thing you should do is seek medical advice. If, however, there is nothing physically wrong with you (and you have a reasonably sensible diet, allowing yourself sufficient time to adequately digest your food) perhaps you should question whether stress is the cause.

Change in eating habits

For some reason stress seems to affect the eating habits of women far more dramatically than those of men. Leaving aside anorexia nervosa (which is always a deep rooted psychological problem, possible causes being an inner fear of growing up or a relationship problem with the mother), any dramatic change in your eating habits can be indicative of an inability to cope with stress. Some women when faced with excessive pressure in their lives cannot eat at all but become members of the 'black coffee and cigarette brigade'; others, however, find that they suddenly develop a constant desire to eat. They find that they will eat anything which happens to be around, even if they are usually quite sensible about their diet.

Alcohol dependency

The important word here is 'dependency'. There is nothing wrong in enjoying the occasional drink. The time to worry is when you start to feel that you cannot cope without that drink. Many women who claim that they would never take tranquillizers or anti-depressants rely on alcohol to help them 'unwind' at the end of the day. Did you know that the technical definition of an alcoholic is someone who *cannot get through the day without one drink?* So look at your drinking habits and see whether alcohol dependency has been creeping up on you.

Pre-menstrual tension (PMT)

Of course there are many reasons why women suffer from pre-menstrual tension (PMT) and not all of them are stress related. It could be that there is a physical cause for the discomfort you feel each month so you would do well to consult your doctor or clinic for advice. But in the vast majority of cases, PMT occurs when a woman is suffering from stress in her everyday life. In any event, whatever the cause of the PMT, it is possible to reduce the pain by means of relaxation exercises.

Pain and discomfort are felt more acutely in muscles which are tensed and stress causes muscular tension so any discomfort which might be present is accentuated. The irritability or extreme sensitivity which many women feel just before the onset of their period can also be alleviated if not eradicated altogether by various forms of relaxation or breathing exercises (details of which appear later in the book).

Asthma and anxiety attacks

I have linked these two symptoms together because they are both based on fluctuations in the emotions. Although an asthmatic may also be susceptible to allergies such as hay fever (which is not stress related), the asthma itself is the result of inner tension. Not only that but fear of an attack also causes great tension in the potential sufferer so that the complaint is often self-perpetuating. It is quite possible to teach an asthmatic to recognise the 'early warning signals' of an attack and at that point – before the attack itself actually arrives on the scene – to take control of the situation and to make the attack disappear before it can take hold. This knowledge that she is in complete control is often sufficient in itself to dramatically reduce the number of threatened attacks.

Anxiety attacks are very frightening to the sufferer. Sometimes their cause is obvious – when a shy or nervous person has to enter a room full of strangers, for example – but at other times the attack itself appears to have no direct cause. You can be sure, however, that there is a cause and that it is definitely related to an accumulation of stress. The fact that the panic occurs at a time when there is no immediately obvious stressful situation merely indicates that the build up of tension has been so great that it only takes some minor incident to trigger it off.

Dizziness and spots before the eyes

If the room seems to spin when you stand up suddenly or turn your head quickly, or if you experience moments when you have spots before your eyes, you are likely to be suffering from a raised level of blood pressure, which in turn is often caused by stress. It is interesting to measure someone's blood pressure before and after a session of relaxation and see just how rapidly it is possible for anybody to reduce the level for themselves. And, of course, as we saw earlier, raised blood pressure is one of the results of reacting to stress.

Increase in smoking

You do not need me to tell you that smoking can never be good for you. But if you suddenly find that you are smoking more than ever before or if your immediate reaction to any stressful or upsetting situation is to reach for a cigarette, perhaps it is time to stop and think about what you are doing. We have all heard the person who assures us that she only smokes to 'calm her nerves' but in fact it does no such thing. Indeed, the nicotine contained in the tobacco actually increases the amount of tension in the body. Add to this the tension caused by the fact that smoking is becoming more and more anti-social and the subconscious fear felt by every smoker (even if this is not admitted) that they are doing themselves permanent, even fatal, damage and you will see why a dramatic increase in the number of cigarettes smoked can often indicate an escalation in the amount of stress experienced.

Permanent feelings of tiredness

We all know when we feel tired because we have been doing too much on a particular day or because we went to bed very late last night and that sort of tiredness is not really a problem. But there is another type of tiredness – a mental and physical exhaustion which never seems to leave you – and that is far more worrying. If you find that you never have any energy, that you cannot face the ordinary tasks of the day or that you are even tired when you wake in the morning, then it is quite likely that you are reacting adversely to the amount of stress in your life.

Aches and pains

Because one of the reactions to a stressful situation is for the muscles to tense in order to be ready for action, if that tension is not then released from the body (either by the action itself, by therapeutic massage or by deliberate relaxation) then you are bound to suffer from assorted aches and pains. So if you find that you frequently have an aching back, a stiff neck, a tense jaw – or a frayed temper – recognise these symptoms as a warning that you need to do something to eliminate some of the stress from your life.

Nervous habits

I do not suppose that anyone ever died from biting their nails any more than from constantly drumming their fingers on the table – unless of course it so infuriated someone else that he or she was driven to violent action! But, minor as they may seem, these habits, like those of grinding your teeth or continuously tapping your foot, are signs that you are under pressure and that you are suffering from stress to a greater or lesser degree. It could be that you are suffering in other ways which you have not even realised are the results of stress. Perhaps it is time to take a look at your life and see what can be done to reduce the amount of stress in it.

Allergies

Many people suffer from allergies of one sort or another all their lives and these do not necessarily have anything to do with stress, although you will usually find that the allergic reactions are more noticeable when the sufferer is going through a particularly stressful period. But if you have always been free of such symptoms and yet you find that you are becoming less and less able to eat particular foods or to touch particular substances, or if you can no longer tolerate bright lights – and if your doctor can find no reason for such changes – it is probable that your body is reacting to excessive stress in your life. Keep a diary and note when your allergic reactions seem to be most severe – and then ask yourself whether you were suffering from any extra pressure at that particular time.

Indigestion

The odd isolated incidence of indigestion is nothing to worry about. But, if you find that you are suffering almost permanently, the first thing you should do is to have a physical check-up as indigestion can, of course, be a symptom of something much more serious such as heart disease. But what if you have a medical check-up only to be told that there is nothing whatsoever wrong with your heart? Indigestion can indicate that you should have a look at your diet but, in addition, it is often the result of stress itself or of the fact that someone who is under extreme pressure tends to gulp food down (or to miss meals altogether) rather than sitting down and enjoying a relaxed and healthy snack.

Frigidity

A woman's hormones can be greatly affected by the amount of stress in her life – and of course your hormones have a direct effect upon your responses to any emotional situation. No one is expecting you to be a permanent Lolita, but if you find that you are becoming less able to respond to sexual stimulation from your partner – and if there is no obvious physical reason – try and reduce either the amount of stress in your life or the way in which you react to it.

Even when you are able to respond sexually and emotionally, an inability to conceive is recognised as being one of the results of excessive tension. We have all heard of the woman who longs so desperately for a child that the stress caused by that very longing is enough to make conception difficult if not impossible. What is not always realised is that *any* extreme stress, whatever the cause, is going to bring about the same result.

Ulcers

At one time thought of as a 'man's complaint', it is now acknowledged that an increasing number of women are suffering from ulcers. It is not only the eating habits of the individual which are to blame, although these may well have to be adjusted after the onset of an ulcer. Stress is often the direct cause and all the changes of diet in the world will not help in the long term if nothing is done about that underlying problem.

High blood pressure

Permanently raised blood pressure is a cause for serious concern and you should always seek medical advice for this complaint. However it has been proved that it is possible to lower the level of the blood pressure in a matter of minutes when following certain relaxation routines. This, of course, only deals with the problem at that particular moment and a routine would have to be followed regularly if you are to deal with the root cause.

Tendency to accidents

We have already seen how one of the reactions to stress is tension of the muscles in readiness to deal with a flight or fight situation. When the situation does not occur, however, the tension in the muscles remains. Anyone whose muscles are permanently tensed is far more likely to have an accident and, what is worse, anyone whose muscles are tensed is far more likely to suffer serious injury in that accident. Little children who fall over seldom do themselves any great harm because their bodies are relaxed. But if an adult suffers a fall, his body is far more likely to be tense and therefore he will usually hurt himself.

Skin complaints

Even when such conditions as rashes, eczema and psoriasis are not caused directly by stress, they are frequently aggravated by it. And because these conditions are distressing in themselves, often of unsightly appearance (although the sufferer is usually far more conscious of this than anyone else) and accompanied by severe irritation, they are not only exacerbated by stress but they perpetuate it. It has been found that psoriasis and eczema are often to be found in people – and women in particular – who appear to cope so remarkably well with any problem which may arise that no one realises that they are suffering from stress at all. It is no coincidence that when such people are taken into hospital for treatment the skin problems seem to disappear as if by magic. All that has happened is that the individual is removed from the stresses in his or her life; there is nothing he can do about any of his usual problems from his hospital bed and so the pressure is relieved and the skin complaint disappears.

Phobias

I am not concerned here with the woman who has suffered from a particular phobia since early childhood, although that condition too is made worse by stress and can be successfully treated by hypnosis among other therapies. The phobias I refer to are those which seem to appear from nowhere – perhaps a sudden onset of agoraphobia or claustrophobia in someone who has never suffered from such a thing before. In many cases you will find that the cause of the phobia is not the obvious one – the agoraphobic is not really terrified of going out of the house – but her mind is reacting to her inner feelings of stress by forcing her to give up what she has been doing in her life and thereby compelling her to reduce the amount of external pressure felt. It is unfortunate, of course, that phobias bring with them their own feelings of stress, often caused because the sufferer feels ridiculous at being unable to cope with a 'normal' situation.

Addiction to prescribed drugs

You must understand that here I am talking only about pre-scribed drugs. This section has nothing to do with addiction to such substances as heroin or cocaine: these are serious conditions which always need professional help. As a hypno-therapist I spend a great deal of my time helping people, usually women, to cut down on the anti-depressants and tranquillizers to which they have become addicted over the years. When doctors first prescribed such pills many years ago they had no idea of the Pandora's box they were opening. I am happy to say that many doctors are now very wary indeed of prescribing these drugs for more than a very limited period of time – and this is just how it should be. It is a fact that anti-depressants cease to have any beneficial effect after a comparatively short period of time and, even in the beginning, they are more likely to mask symptoms than to effect a cure.

It is important to remember one thing and that is if you happen to be addicted to any form of anti-depressant or tranquillizer, whether prescribed or purchased over the counter, you must *never* simply stop taking them. The symptoms which would follow such action could be both harmful and distressing. But as you learn to reduce the amount of stress in your life, it should be possible to cut down the tablets very gradually until you are eventually able to do without them.

Irritability and anger

Your partner promises to be home at 7.30pm and it is 9pm before you hear his key in the lock. For an hour and a half you have imagined him lying splattered on some road as the result of a terrible accident. You are relieved and happy when he arrives home, but what do you do? You scream and shout at him, displaying all the signs of anger rather than relief. That is just one incident but if your life is full of stressful situations you may find that you are becoming more irritable or bad tempered with each day that passes. You may not even become aware of this change in your temperament until it is pointed out to you. A frustrated infant will relieve his feelings by screaming his head off, but we 'civilised' individuals are not allowed to indulge in such dramatic displays. So we do the next best thing, we become angry over trifles which in less tense times would not have bothered us greatly. In extreme cases that anger may turn to violence – mental or physical – bringing even more havoc in its wake. Far better, if you feel the pressure building up within you, to find some other way of releasing all those pent up feelings of frustration. Smash a tennis ball, dig the garden or work off that excess energy by running for a mile or two. Much better, you may think, than allowing yourself to take out your feelings on those around you, often causing irreparable damage to personal relationships.

Strokes and heart disease

There was a time when most strokes or heart attacks seemed to be suffered by men. But with the rise in the number of women who work that situation has changed. The sufferer from extreme stress could be the career woman, working her way up the corporate ladder or the shop assistant trying to cope with the demands of home and job. A single stressful incident is unlikely to bring about either a stroke or the onset of coronary disease but an accumulation of incidents over a long period of time can certainly do so. In no way is this claim intended to frighten you; merely to show you the wisdom of dealing with stress before it reaches such gigantic proportions.

Cancer

It is an acknowledged fact that a great many cases of cancer are caused as a result of extreme stress and the inability to cope with situations. If you look at the life of a cancer sufferer about two or three years before the onset of the disease, you will often find that either there has been a situation with which she has been totally unable to cope or else she has coped wonderfully well on the surface while all the time the damage was occurring within her. Now this does not mean that anyone who goes through a trying and stressful period is going to develop cancer two or three years later – of course not. What it does mean is that people whose immune systems may be less efficient or who may react more dramatically to stress are in greater danger of contracting the disease. No one is going to travel happily through life without encountering periods of stress but, provided you have learned how to release it and reduce its harmful effects, you should be able to avoid many of its more serious results.

Look at the following questionnaire. Read the statements contained in it and see whether they apply to you. Remember we are not talking about isolated incidents which can apply to anybody but something which happens regularly. If you can answer 'yes' to a large number of them – and especially if the situation seems to have become more noticeable recently – perhaps it is time for you to do something about the stress factor in your life.

Table 1. Medical stress check

Place a tick against any of the statements which regularly apply to you
I frequently suffer from headaches
I suffer migraine attacks
My eyes are often tired and aching
I find it difficult to take a deep breath
I have a tendency to hyperventilate
I suffer from insomnia
I often wake during the night
I find it difficult to wake in the morning
My dreams are disturbing or distressing
I often suffer from nausea or vomiting
I eat far more than I used to
I eat far less than I used to
I have a craving for sweet foods
I cannot cope without an alcoholic drink
I suffer from PMT
I have painful periods
I have very heavy periods
I have frequent attacks of asthma
I often experience a sense of panic

I am frequently tearful

My heart appears to race

I suffer from dizziness

I often have spots before my eyes

My smoking has increased

I am always tired

I have no energy

My limbs often ache for no known reason

I have several nervous habits

I bite my nails

I am becoming allergic to more substances

I often suffer from indigestion

I am frequently constipated

I often have diarrhoea

I have lost all interest in sex

I am unable to respond during sexual intercourse

My doctor has diagnosed an ulcer

My blood pressure is regularly high

I suffer from irrational fears

I have become accident prone

I suffer from eczema or psoriasis

I am addicted to medication

I am often irritable or short-tempered

I frequently feel strong anger

I am tempted to be violent

I regularly suffer from pains in the chest
My neck and back muscles often ache

In addition to all the physical reactions to stress mentioned in the questionnaire above, there are a multitude of emotional symptoms which are quite definitely stress-related. Study the statements in Table 2 and see how many of them apply to you.

Table 2. Emotional stress check

Place a tick against any of the following statements which you feel apply to you
I have a permanent feeling of anxiety
I do not have a very high opinion of myself
It is difficult to concentrate for any length of time
I cannot generate much enthusiasm
My memory is getting worse
Other people often let me down
I do not like myself very much
In general, I think I am a failure
I feel apathetic towards life
I never feel at ease with others
I am not able to relax
I find it difficult to cope with life
Displaying emotion is hard for me
I cannot demonstrate physical affection
It is difficult for me to tell others how I feel
I often feel anger which I suppress
My fears are not always logical

In general I am a restless person
I suffer from feelings of guilt about the past
I fear being ill
I am afraid of dying
I cannot bear ill health in others
The future frightens me
I feel oppressed in enclosed spaces
I feel anxious in open spaces
Other people always put the blame on me
People expect more of me than I can give
I am not generally liked by other people
I am often misunderstood
I do not have much patience
I like to do several things at once
I lack self confidence

Please do not be disheartened, even if quite a number of the statements contained in the two questionnaires seem to apply to you. The situation can easily be improved. Indeed the very fact that you are reading this book shows that you are aware of the problems stress causes in women and that you wish to do something about it. The following chapters will show you just how stressful situations arise. In as many cases as possible they will also show you what you can do to prevent or minimise them. Because there will always be certain circumstances in our lives about which we can do nothing, the final chapter will show you some simple ways in which you can safeguard yourself against the effects of stress, ways which you can put into practice straight away.

2

Girls Will Be Girls

No woman today would really want to return to the conditions which existed in the time of our grandmothers and yet perhaps in some ways things were easier for women then. They had no real decisions to make about the way in which they were going to live their lives. For the most part each woman would grow up to marry, run a home, bear and raise children. The ease or difficulty of such a life, of course, depended greatly upon their financial status and whether or not they were able to afford domestic help. Women who did not marry still did not have much of a choice. If they were educated and of a 'certain class', they would probably go on to work as governesses or companions; if not, many would be likely to spend their days in domestic service.

Although to women of today the life of a servant in the early part of this century would appear to be one of misery and drudgery, the servants themselves did not always consider it so. Some nine years ago I was introduced to Annie Brigg, a delightful lady who was then in her late seventies. As the oldest of a family of eight children, Annie had left home to go into service when she was just eleven years old. I spent a fascinating evening listening to her tales of 'the big house' and her duties there. She told me of the life below stairs and of her progress from having to do the most menial of tasks to becoming personal maid to the daughter of the household which position remained hers until she married when she was twenty-six. One would think that this must have been for Annie a most miserable existence but she had not found it so. She had been happy to find work which meant that she need no longer be a burden on her family. She was housed, clothed and fed and, although the work was hard – particularly in the beginning – she had enjoyed the company of her extended 'family' (the other servants) and had been well treated by her employers. At no time had it occurred to her to question the justice of the employer/servant position and indeed, even looking back on it many decades later, she had no regrets about her early life. In fact she considered herself one of the lucky ones.

Although the situation for women improved somewhat as time went on, even those little girls born forty years ago became part of the 'Janet and John syndrome'. The majority of them were brought up to have very fixed ideas about their tasks in life. As children they would help their mothers, learning to cook, sew and generally keep house while their brothers were out there helping their fathers look after the garden. As they grew older they expected that, although they might have a job after leaving school, they would eventually marry – and would stay married. It is not so many years ago that, if you knew someone who had been divorced, the matter was gossiped about in whispered tones. I realise, of course, that I am generalising and that there always were and always will be exceptions to the norm. Indeed, many of those young women who spoke so scathingly of divorce were later to experience it for themselves.

ALLOWING YOURSELF TO BE FEMININE

From the days when girls 'knew their place' we now seem to have gone to the other extreme. The more ardent feminists do all that they can to persuade women that not only should they be allowed to compete with men but that they *must* do so. This is all very well for those who wish to be car mechanics or to work on oil rigs – and indeed if they are capable of doing such a job they should be allowed to – but what of those other women, the ones who, whether as a result of personal choice or unavoidable circumstances, decide to remain in the home and look after their children or who wish to follow what are more usually considered to be 'feminine pursuits'. Why should these women be made to feel guilty?

Case Study: Janice

Janice is an intelligent and well-educated young woman. After leaving school she went on to university where she gained a second class degree in English. She married Don when she was just twenty-four and continued with her work as a researcher/personal assistant to an eminent travel writer until the birth of her first child, three years after her marriage. Her second baby was born some two years later. Having no real financial worries, Janice decided that she would remain at home caring for husband and family until her younger child started senior school at eleven years old. It was always at the back of her mind that she would then return to work but she was not anxious for a demanding career and in the meantime her chosen life made her happy and fulfilled. She had her own friends, in addition to those she and Don knew as a couple. She joined a discussion group, went to the theatre, read widely and had time to indulge in her hobby of painting. She was content.

As time went on, however, the situation changed. More and more articles appeared in magazines which seemed to condemn those women who, having had a reasonable education, chose to stay at home and 'vegetate'. The media in general appeared to be condemning women like Janice, accusing them of being society's parasites. Very soon it seemed to Janice that, whenever she was introduced to someone new, the first question she would be asked was 'What do you do?' She began to feel guilty and inadequate as though not only was she wasting her own intelligence but she was letting down women in general. Much as she loved Don and her children, she subconsciously began to resent them as if, in some way, they were the cause of the problem. And because her common sense told her that this was not really so, she began to feel even more guilty. She tried to reconcile her own wishes with what she felt – and, even more significantly, with what other people felt she *should* be doing

As the tension built up Janice started to sleep badly; it seemed that, even when she went to bed, she could not stop turning things over in her mind although she did not feel able to come to any conclusions or make any firm decisions. Her relationship with her husband deteriorated because, knowing that they were unjustified, she kept her feelings of resentment bottled up within her. Don had always been supportive and she knew that he would continue to be so if she decided to go back to work; they could even afford the extra help to make such a step easy for her. But the resentment was there nonetheless and soon she even found herself unable to respond to Don physically, almost as though she was blaming him for the entire situation. It was at this stage that Janice came to see me.

I urged Janice to study her life carefully and to ask herself the following questions.

Had she chosen her way of life? The answer was definitely 'yes'. She had made a deliberate decision when expecting her first child to remain at home and bring them up herself. Her husband had been happy for her to do so.

Did she feel the decision was good for the children? Once again, yes. She was able to give them more of her time than would have been possible, even had she only had a part time job. She had been there to help them develop – she had even taught the older one to read. They went for interesting walks together, played together, learned together and she was there to answer their questions as and when they arose.

Had she the opportunity to use her mind and her intelligence? In addition to her discussion group, her outings to the theatre and her books, Janice had a number of good friends with whom she could converse and, until recently when relations had become more strained, she and Don had always discussed things together.

Was her decision causing hardship to anyone else? She was hurting no one by choosing to remain at home. Don had a successful career and the family had no financial problems. Even if she decided to get a job, she knew that the greater part of her income would be swallowed up by having to employ help in the house or with the children and, having less time at home, by the use of more convenience foods and so on.

Was her present frame of mind damaging her relationship with her husband? Janice had to admit that this was so. Because she had felt unable to discuss her inner feelings with Don he could not understand why she was becoming more irritable and less interested in the physical side of their relationship. The situation then caused him anxiety so that he, in his turn, became silent and uneasy. The rift between them seemed to be widening daily.

I could have gone on from this point to ask Janice to list all the advantages and disadvantages of her way of life based on her answers to these questions and then to weigh up the situation. However the bottom line was that she still *wanted* to be at home while her children were young. She not only felt that it would be best for them – she really enjoyed it. Having thought the matter through and talked it over, she began to feel better. She was intelligent enough to see that she should not allow herself to be influenced by what other people felt she should be doing.

If you are harbouring feelings of guilt about this or any similar situation, try asking yourself these questions:

* Have I chosen my path either myself or after discussion with someone whose opinion I trust and value?

* Does my choice adversely affect anyone else; if so, in what way?

* If the answer to the above is 'yes', what could I do, within the boundaries imposed by my choice of direction, to improve the situation?

* Is my sense of guilt damaging my relationships with others? If so, in what way? What can I do about it?

* Are my doubts the result of the opinions of other people being forced upon me? If so, do I really want to lead my life the way others think I should?

SEXUALITY AND SOCIETY'S PRESSURES

Not only has there been a considerable amount of indoctrination about the way young girls 'should' behave as they grow up but, in addition, women are bombarded from a very early age with ideas and stories about sexual behaviour. It is a fact that the age of physical maturity for both girls and boys is getting younger. It is also true that both sexes are now much younger when they make that transition from innocence to sexual knowledge.

No one wants to return to the standards of the Victorian era when prudity was at its height and women were expected to be modest and dutiful and to lie back and think of England. It is a good thing that girls are now more aware and less ashamed of their bodies. But is it a good thing that very young girls now have the impression that sex is the be-all and end-all of life thrust at them by the media and by their peers? Children are experimenting with sex at a progressively earlier age – although they do not appear to be taught much about the link between a sexual relationship and the concept of love. Films, books, television programmes – all these have played their part in forcing upon audiences images of promiscuity. And, since all audiences contain a proportion of children, these sources cannot abdicate their responsibilities. From early James Bond films to the advertisements for certain alcoholic drinks, the concept that sex is a desirable end in itself is repeated over and over again. It has taken the AIDS scare for the situation to improve but media sources are responsible for the stress which still exists in many young women who felt that they must be 'different' or unusual because they were not enjoying the highly active sex life which they feel must be the norm.

Case Study: Camilla

By the time Camilla was twenty-one she was terrified even to go out with men. The only child of older parents, she had always been somewhat quiet and shy. At school the other girls had seemed to talk of nothing but boyfriends and sex. Camilla had never been sure that all they said was true but, because it was something in which she had never been involved, she was not quite sure. This feeling that she was missing out on something which she did not quite understand made her feel different to all the other girls in her class; she was unable to join in their chatter and eventually they tended to ignore her altogether. Camilla's confidence spiralled rapidly downwards; she withdrew into a corner with her books, rarely speaking to anyone of her own age. Sadly she never learned how to be a teenager, never was able to join in the banter; she was never invited to parties and never developed an ability to get on with others of her own age. At twenty-one she had never had a real friendship with another girl, let alone a boyfriend.

After leaving school, Camilla went to work as a typist in a busy office but, never having learned to make friends, she led an isolated existence there too. It was not that anyone was actively unpleasant to her, just that they did not seem to notice that she was there. Because she had no one with whom she could have lunch and because she was not really interested in window shopping on her own, Camilla would bring sandwiches to the office and spend her lunch hour with her head buried in a book. Eventually she became aware that someone else stayed in the office at lunchtime too – a young man called Terry who had only recently started to work there. One day Terry began a conversation with Camilla and they soon discovered that they had similar tastes in music and a shared interest in conservation. Their friendship developed slowly until one day Terry asked Camilla if she would care to go to the cinema with him and, somewhat hesitantly, she agreed. She worried for days about her forthcoming 'date' and, when the time came, she was so terrified that Terry might try to make sexual advances towards her that she could hardly speak to him and froze completely when he tried to hold her hand. He never asked her out again.

I realise, of course, that Camilla's case is an extreme one. Nevertheless the difficulties encountered by many women with regard to relationships throughout their lives have their basis in tension caused during their teenage years. Even though an adult can appreciate that we are all bound at some time to have unsuccessful relationships where the fault can be laid at no one's door but is due to the incompatibility of the people involved, a very young woman is always going to wonder if she was to blame. When that young woman is convinced (often wrongly) that everyone else is having a wonderful time, she begins to feel even more inadequate and more of a failure where men are concerned. And so she is trapped on an ever descending spiral. If she has no one with whom she can discuss her fears and her worries, what spheres of influence exist other than the world of entertainment and the media. Even though the more sexually explicit programmes are supposed to be screened after nine o'clock in the evening, there are always the advertisements, the often suggestive pop videos, magazines – and even 'page 3'. And, of course, there is nothing whatsoever to prevent any young person recording a late night programme on a video cassette or indeed hiring a film from their local video club shop.

And so a totally false impression is created of what a woman should be like, of the relationships between men and women and of how the rest of the world is behaving. The Camillas of this world cannot help but ask themselves what everyone else is doing and wondering whether, because she is not doing the same thing, something is dramatically wrong with her.

If you feel that even part of the stress from which you suffer is caused by your relationships with the opposite sex, ask yourself the following questions:

* How do I think a woman should look?

* How do I think a woman should act towards men?

* How should men act towards women?

* On what are my opinions based?

* Do I feel that I am different to other people? Do I feel inferior to others?

* When did these feelings of inferiority start to manifest themselves?

* If it all began when you were at school, look back through the eyes of an intelligent adult. Do you really believe that everything you heard there was true?

* If you feel that you were influenced by the media, ask yourself whether you really believe all that you read, saw or heard.

* Would I like a relationship with a man?

* Remembering that, just as all women are different, all men are different (in other words, some prefer one type of woman and some another), ask yourself whether you really believe that all men are the same. Think of the different men you know, whether members of the family or acquaintances; they all have different personalities therefore it follows that they all want different things.

FEAR OF ATTACK

As women are becoming stronger in some ways, so they appear to be growing more vulnerable in others. One of the major causes of stress in women today is the fear of attack – this affects everyone from the very young to the very old. There is no way that you can guarantee that you are not going to be attacked or robbed, but there is certainly a great deal you can do to make it a lot less likely and therefore to reduce the amount of stress caused by your fears.

It is a proven fact that the majority of physical attacks upon women take place in the home and the attacker is often someone whom the victim has voluntarily allowed into her home. (I am not dealing here with violence within the family which is a separate issue entirely). There are, therefore, several steps you can take which will make this less likely to happen.

Make sure who is at the door

1.   It should be stating the obvious to ask you to check the identification of any official who may knock at your door. All meter readers, repair men, police and so on, carry identification cards and none of them will mind you looking at them closely and even telephoning their office if you have any doubts in your mind at all. It is not wise to rely simply on the fact that your caller is wearing a uniform as these are not difficult for the unscrupulous to obtain.

2.   If someone calls at your house unexpectedly and you do not have a glass panel or a window through which you can see who it is, never hesitate to call through a closed door and ask who it is. If you do decide to open the door, particularly at night, it is wise to do so with the safety chain in position. No friend will be at all offended if you do so as they will quite understand the reason.

Safeguard your home

1. Ensure that there are adequate locks and bolts on any external doors and ground floor windows. If you have any doubts about what type of locks to fix, your local police Crime Prevention Officer will be happy to visit and advise you.
2. Fix an external light to the front of your house. A simple porch light is better than nothing but even more effective are the sensitive lights which come on automatically as soon as anyone comes near. This will not only deter unwelcome intruders but is very useful for you if you are returning home after dark.
3. Time switches are relatively inexpensive and, fitted to lights both upstairs and down, can make it seem as though someone is in the house even if you are still at work or even away on holiday.
4. Never leave ladders in easily accessible positions in the garden even when decorating is in progress. It is well worth the time and trouble of removing any form of stepladder at the end of each working day if this is going to deter unwelcome visitors.

Don't take unnecessary risks

1. If you are alone, never take short cuts if they involve going down dark alleys or through undesirable areas, particularly at night.
2. If your car breaks down and you are forced to stop, particularly if this happens on a motorway or a lonely road:
a) If someone pulls up and offers to help you, open the window *just a crack* and ask him if he will telephone for help on your behalf. (It is often wise to ask this of two or three different people as the first one may not bother.) According to the police, if you do decide to accept an offer of help, it is preferable to accept it from a lorry driver rather than a car driver. This is because all lorries and their drivers are registered and their journeys logged and monitored whereas a car driver need not even be the owner of the vehicle.
b) Keep a rolled-up sheet of drawing paper in your car on which you have written in large, clear letters: 'I HAVE BROKEN DOWN. PLEASE TELEPHONE FOR HELP.' There are such signs available commercially specifically for this purpose, but it is just as easy to make your own.

3.   If you have to walk through a built-up area at night to get to your destination, your parked car or your bus stop, try and keep to the brightest side of the street. If there are no brightly lit shop windows, then walk under the street lamps where possible.

If you are stopped in the street

1.   If all that he wants is your money – give it to him! No possession is worth fighting and being injured for. But give yourself time to escape by throwing your handbag on the ground so that your challenger has to turn and pick it up. If it is your jewellery he wants, take it off and throw that down too, for the same reason. Money, credit cards, cheque books, jewellery – all these are all replaceable. You are not.
2.   Having tossed your valuables in his direction, run to the nearest house showing a light (preferably downstairs) and bang at the door. Instead of shouting 'Help', 'Attack', 'Rape' or 'Robbery' – which might make the people in the house choose not to hear you – try yelling 'Fire' instead. That will make them come to the door.

If you are attacked

1.   You are the only one who can make the decision whether or not to allow the attack (particularly if it is sexual) to continue. It may be that you feel you will suffer less harm if you do not offer any resistance. You, and only you, have the right to make that decision and I would not seek to sway you one way or the other.
2.   If you decide to fight, remember that you have to do two things. The first move is to defend yourself and the second is to prevent your attacker following you while you make your escape. That means that you have to hurt him and, while I am not normally in favour of violence, my own view is that anyone who attempts to violate your person deserves whatever he gets. Since the attacker is likely to be a young man who may well be able to run faster than you, you want to cause him instant pain rather than permanent damage so it is probably best to aim for the eyes, the ears, the knees or the genitals.

There are, in fact, several organisations up and down the country who give lessons in practical self defence for women.

These are designed to help you escape from an unpleasant situation not to turn you into a fearless commando or a karate expert.

3. Have you ever wondered why some people are mugged, attacked, robbed or even raped several times while others never seem to have a problem? It seems as though certain people give off negative vibrations or an aura of fear which is subconsciously recognised by their would-be attackers. If we can accept that dogs can sense fear in humans, why should it not be possible for other humans to sense it too? So, within the boundaries of common sense and taking whatever precautions you can, try to be as calm and relaxed as possible in any situation and you will be less likely to attract negative reactions on the part of others.

WOMEN AND AIDS

Another aspect of relationships which has recently been causing a great deal of stress in many women is the problem of AIDS.

Case study: Marianne

Marianne divorced her husband about seven years ago. Since that time she has had one serious relationship which ended after fifteen months. Six months later she went on holiday to Venice and it was there that she met Paulo, an attractive Italian some five years her junior. They had a typically intense holiday romance which both of them knew would not become anything more permanent and this romance, not unusually, led to Marianne having a sexual relationship with her Italian lover.

At the time the thought of AIDS (or any other sexually transmitted disease) did not even enter Marianne's head. It was only when she returned home and confided in her best friend that Amy said, quite seriously, 'I hope you made sure he used a condom'. From that moment Marianne began to worry. She tried to put the matter out of her mind but she became more and more troubled. Eventually she was unable to eat, to sleep or to concentrate on her job. Finally she went to a clinic for tests – and then went to hell and back while waiting for the results. Fortunately all was well.

Many women are finding themselves in an intolerably difficult position and they do not know what to do for the best. It may be that the couple having a 'fling' at the office party find it easier to talk of using a condom than the couple setting out on what they hope will be a long term or permanent relationship. If the man does not suggest using any protection, what is the woman to do? If she asks him to do so, it may appear that she is casting doubts upon his morals but if she does not, she may be condemning herself to a prolonged period of worry. It is not easy in the throes of a newly aroused passion to say 'Wait a minute; have you got a condom handy?' And if the woman suddenly produces one from her handbag she may worry in case the man thinks she always carries them because of her promiscuous nature.

Of course this problem is not only caused by passionate temporary affairs or brand new relationships. What of the woman who suspects that her partner is being unfaithful? Not only does she have the doubt and possible emotional hurt, but now she has the added worry that he could transmit to her a potentially life-threatening condition.

If you find yourself in this highly stressful situation, ask yourself the following question:

* Which is more frightening: the thought of a few moments embarrassment or months of worry and anxiety culminating hopefully in relief but possibly in a death sentence?

GOING IT ALONE

There are, of course, many women in this increasingly emancipated age who have no desire at all to be involved in an emotional or physical relationship.

Case Study: Karen

Karen is forty-six and has been divorced for nine years. Her three children are all living away from home; one is at university and the other two are working in other parts of the country. She has a responsible senior management position in a large financial corporation where she is greatly respected for her ability. She is on friendly terms with both her male and female colleagues at her place of work and, in addition, she has a full and enjoyable social life. Although, as Karen herself put it, she might well be tempted if 'Mr Wonderful' were to arrive on the scene, unless that actually happens she is really not interested in a permanent relationship involving long term commitment; she is happy with her life the way it is.

During the time she has been working at the company, two or three of her colleagues have asked her out – and indeed she had two very enjoyable dinners, a visit to the cinema and one to a concert. But once she made it clear to the gentlemen concerned that, although she liked them and valued their friendship, she was not looking for a deeper relationship, she was never asked again. One man even complained that, because Karen had obviously made an effort to look nice for their outing and yet she had then said 'no', she was obviously a tease. Another actually accused her of being a lesbian – implying presumably that there could be no other reason for her failing to acknowledge his obvious charms. The situation imposed a great deal of stress on Karen who then felt unable to mix socially with her colleagues on friendly terms although this was what she wanted.

Protecting yourself

I am not pretending that there is an easy answer to any of these problems. There is not a great deal that you can do to change the attitudes of others – only the passage of time and increased understanding can do that. What you can change is the way in which you allow those attitudes to affect you and whether or not you permit yourself to suffer from stress because of them.

3

Decisions, Decisions

The educational system today seems to demand specialisation at a progressively early age. Children are expected to select the subjects they wish to study (and on which their future careers may well be based) soon after they have reached senior school level. This is often a time when they may still be greatly influenced by the hopes and desires of their family. 'We have always been involved in the medical profession – of course Samantha will go on to be a doctor'; 'Jeremy is certain to go into the army, like his father and grandfather before him'; 'It doesn't really matter which exams Derek takes – he will be joining us in the family business'. The situation is bad enough for boys but it is even worse for girls. From the moment she is asked to choose the subjects for her examinations at school, life for a woman today is one long round of decisions. Not only does she have to make up her mind what *she* wants; in many cases she also has to do battle with the pre-conceived ideas of parents or teachers. There are still some families where the parents do not consider it worth while for a girl to continue with higher education, believing that her only real purpose in life is to be a wife and mother. And even among those families where it is accepted that a girl will want – and is entitled to – a career of her own, it is often felt that, although this whim might be indulged, the career will only be a stop gap, something with which to fill the intervening period between leaving college and getting married.

KIDS AND CAREER?

Now all this is fine for those girls who want nothing more in life than marriage and motherhood, and no one is to say that they are wrong for having these aims. And the situation, though likely to be more difficult, will not affect the long term plans of those girls who are determined to carve out careers for themselves and whose concepts of the future do not include motherhood. But what about the majority of young women, the ones who would like to feel that a committed relationship, and possibly children, will figure somewhere in their future but who are determined to work towards an interesting and fulfilling career in the meantime?

Case Study: Elaine

Elaine had done well in school from the very beginning. She was a bright, lively and intelligent girl who, while studying for her A-levels, was looking forward to going on to university and having a worthwhile career thereafter. Her father, however, was firmly set against the idea. A hardworking man who had always done his best for his wife and family, he still clung to the traditional concepts with which he had been brought up – that a woman's place was in the home and that further education was for men only. Oh, it would be all very well for Elaine to work as a typist or a shop assistant after leaving school – after all, it was about time that she made some contribution to the family finances – but he felt that she should put all this education nonsense right out of her mind.

Elaine tried to reason with her father but all to no avail. She knew there was no point in attempting to enlist the aid of her mother, a gentle, loving but rather timid woman who was still somewhat bemused by talk of universities and degrees. Even if her mother had not agreed with her father, she would still have backed him up, as that was the pattern of their marriage. And, of course the extra money would come in handy.

Having no one else to turn to, Elaine sought the help of her headmistress who managed to persuade the girl's parents to allow her to attend the university interviews. When, after achieving excellent results in her A-level examinations, Elaine was offered places at no less than three different colleges, once again it was the headmistress who stepped into the breach and convinced her father (much against what he felt was his better judgement), that she should be allowed to take up the place of her choice. And so Elaine finally had her wish and went off to study sociology and economics at university.

However, instead of life becoming easier, Elaine found that she was faced with even more problems. She did not know what to do for the best. When vacation time came she never knew whether or not to go home and see her parents. She had never found it easy to communicate with her father and now it was harder than ever. He criticised her for using 'fancy words' and accused his daughter of considering herself 'too good for the rest of us now'. But if, for any reason, Elaine was not able to go home on a regular basis, he told his wife that their daughter 'doesn't want to know us any more'. Elaine found that life at her family home was becoming so intolerable that she began to look for excuses to stay away. Then, of course, she felt even more guilty.

There is not a great deal you can do to alter the firmly held convictions of those around you. If you try persuasion and reasoning but without success, all you can do is make sure that their attitudes do not cause you undue stress. In the end there is little you can do except accept the situation. How another person chooses to act, although naturally based upon the influences of their particular upbringing and experiences, is their own responsibility. The views of Elaine's father may have been the result of the ideas held by those around him during his earlier life. But the fact that he was unwilling even to discuss the matter or try to understand, even if not to agree with, his daughter's viewpoint was entirely his own decision. Had Elaine allowed herself to suffer because of the stress of the situation, she would not have changed his views or improved the position in any way. So she did the only thing she felt she was able to do. She went on with her own life at university, and enjoyed it thoroughly. She kept in regular contact with her parents and visited them from time to time, doing her best to avoid all contentious topics of conversation when she did so.

JUGGLING WORK WITH A RELATIONSHIP

Once a woman with a good job or a burgeoning career becomes involved in a serious relationship involving commitment on both sides she will often find that she is faced with one decision after another. Life is somewhat simpler for the woman whose greatest desire is to be a wife and mother, either staying at home and caring for her family or working at a job which does not tax her too much and which certainly plays quite a minor role in her life – often being seen merely as a source of additional income rather than as being of any intrinsic value. But what is the career-minded woman to do when torn between her work and her relationship?

Case Study: Suzanne

Suzanne was initially employed as a sales representative by a large organisation specialising in the manufacture and distribution of health foods. She had proved to be so good at her job that she was very soon promoted to a senior position with responsibility for the training and supervision of quite a large sales force. This involved a good deal of travelling around the country, staying in hotels two or three nights a week. Suzanne loved the life. She knew that she was good at her job – the results proved that. She enjoyed the responsibility that went with her position, the company of her colleagues and the itinerant lifestyle. She also enjoyed an excellent salary, a company car and the opportunity to stay in some excellent hotels.

Then she met and fell in love with Clive, a music teacher at the local senior school. After a while they decided to set up home together and, because Suzanne never seemed to have time to go house hunting, the simplest solution seemed to be for Clive to move into her comfortable flat in the centre of town.

Throughout their courtship and when they first started to live together Clive always seemed to be very proud of Suzanne and what she had achieved. He did not envy her in any way as he would not have cared at all for the type of work she was doing. Eventually, however, he grew to resent her prolonged absences and the fact that, even when she was at home, she always brought a mountain of paperwork back to the flat and spent most of the evening working on it. He began to complain about the fact that, while he was at home early almost every evening, Suzanne hardly ever seemed to be there – she was either working late or staying in a hotel many miles away. He felt that his idea of a shared life was obviously very different from hers. Being quieter and more introverted than Suzanne, he did not have much of a social life, tending to stay at home alone listening to music and it only served to increase his feelings of resentment that he knew she was enjoying the social side of her work, mixing with the other salespeople in hotel bars and lounges.

Suzanne could not understand his attitude at all. After all, as she pointed out to him, Clive had always known about her career and how much it meant to her. He had never given any indication that he resented it or the amount of time she had to devote to it and she had never given him reason to think that she would change the responsibilities of her work when he moved in with her.

She tried to explain to him just how important her career was to her and how proud she was of the way she had risen within the company. She loved Clive but she had no intention of giving up her work just because he wanted her to. In addition she had a very good income – better than his in fact – and this would help them to save for the type of house they had both decided they would like.

At first Clive appeared to be somewhat appeased and to accept her reassurances but he soon reverted to his old ways, becoming progressively morose and resentful. Finally he issued an ultimatum: he was no longer prepared to be a 'career widower' so Suzanne must either find a local job, change her work altogether or they must split up.

Suzanne's first reaction was to refuse outright – but she really did love Clive so eventually she compromised and changed her job to one which did not involve so much travelling or staying away from home. For the first few months 'playing house' was something of a novelty to her but gradually she began to feel increasingly resentful of the fact that she was not using her full potential – nor, indeed, was she earning the money to which she had become accustomed. Although the final decision to change jobs had been hers, she knew that she would never have done so had it not been for Clive's ultimatum and she began to feel anger and bitterness towards him. She was able to suppress these feelings initially but eventually they showed in her attitude towards him. The relationship began to deteriorate dramatically, although they actually stayed together for another four years.

What could Suzanne and Clive have done to sort out their differences with the minimum of friction?

Discuss the situation at the right moment They had certainly discussed the situation – over and over again. But it had usually been at a time when built-up resentment was ready to make one or other of them explode with anger. Things were said and accusations hurled which would never have been uttered had they tried to talk about things at a time when they were calm. If there is a deep-seated difference of opinion between you and your partner, you will never improve the situation by trying to sort it out when one or both of you is suffering from an accumulation of stress and resentment.

Weigh up the pros and cons There is a great deal to be said for making lists! If Suzanne and Clive had each made lists of the advantages and disadvantages of their way of life and then compared the two, it is possible that they would have found quite a number of areas of agreement – or certainly of compromise.

Compromise if you can While every one of us would like to live our lives in our own way, once you are committed to another person there is always going to be a certain amount of compromise. Perhaps Clive would have been happier for things to continue as they were if it had been agreed that, once they had sufficient money for the house they wanted, Suzanne would be willing to find a job which did not entail the same amount of travelling. Most situations are bearable if you know that they will come to an end at some specific time in the future.

Once a decision has been reached, accept it gracefully Obviously it is up to each of the two individuals concerned to accept or reject whatever suggestion is put forward. But, once a decision is made or a compromise reached, each of them should do their best to accept it and to go forward without bitterness or resentment. In the case of Suzanne and Clive, the end result was two unhappy people. Having given up the job she loved, Suzanne's anger and resentment had caused her to destroy the relationship for which she had made the sacrifice. And by allowing himself to become embittered by the amount of time Suzanne devoted to her work, Clive had allowed himself to issue an ultimatum – never a basis for a happy relationship.

Case Study: Margie

Margie had been working as a typist in the office of a small local firm when she was introduced to Dave at a friend's birthday party. They were immediately attracted to one another and became engaged just a few weeks later, marrying the following year. Margie had none of Suzanne's problems as she had never had any desire for a career but was quite content to work at her job, doing her best while she was in the office but putting it right out of her mind once she left at the end of the day. She and Dave decided to postpone having a family until they had their own home – after all, she was only twenty-two so there was plenty of time. They saved hard and finally bought a small but pretty house on a new estate just outside town.

They were both still young and so it seemed only sensible for Margie to continue working until they had decorated the house, bought a washing machine and had a decent holiday. Then they felt that perhaps their little house would be too small for the three or four children they had agreed they would like. Now they had to decide whether they should both continue to work until they had sufficient money for a larger house. This would entail a larger mortgage and there was no way that Dave could afford that on his earnings alone. If Margie were to become pregnant and leave work now, they would never be able to move. They decided that they would save all that they could and move as soon as possible so that they could start their longed-for family.

They moved into their new home when Margie was just thirty. They stopped using birth control and waited for the inevitable pregnancy. But the inevitable did not happen. As the months turned into a year Margie became more and more anxious about the situation. She wanted to have children while she was still young enough to cope. By the time she was thirty-two, Margie was beginning to feel that time was running out as she would have liked a large family and she had no desire to be a pensioner by the time the youngest child left home. They consulted doctors, saw specialists and had tests – but still nothing happened. All the doctors would say was that they were 'trying too hard' and that was causing Margie a great deal of stress – and tension of any sort makes conception far less likely. That, of course, is one of the classic statements which are easy to make but about which it is very hard to do anything. Eventually Margie went to a therapist to deal with the stress and eighteen months later she was overjoyed to discover that she was pregnant.

It is, of course, well known to most people that stress can make conception extremely difficult. There are innumerable cases of women who, having given up all hope of pregnancy, have adopted a child only to discover that they have conceived a short time later – when the stress of trying has disappeared. Margie had never doubted that she would be able to have a child and so, when nothing happened within the first few months although she desperately wanted to have several children, she began to panic. The stress built up with each month that passed and before long Margie was trapped within that all too common vicious circle.

We can wonder whether Margie and Dave should have been content with their small house – after all many children are brought up happily and satisfactorily in small houses – or whether they were right to want something more for themselves and their future family. Each individual couple must come to their own conclusion. Perhaps it would have been possible for them to start their family while in their first little house and for Margie to have gone back to work at a later date in order to help with the financial burden of an increased mortgage. The most important point to make here, as in the case of Suzanne and Clive, is that whatever decision is reached no good will come of allowing tension to build up because of it. For Margie that tension almost robbed her of the chance of the family she longed for.

An entirely different set of problems, and therefore decisions, face the dedicated career woman who cannot make up her mind whether or not she wants to have children. Biological make up plus centuries of indoctrination combine to convince many women that they should have children if at all possible. It is only in very recent years that some women have had the courage – for courage is what it takes – to make it known that, even if they are part of a secure and loving relationship, they have no desire to give birth to or bring up a family of their own. It is perhaps too soon to know how many of those women come later to regret their decision.

For every one who is able to make a definite decision that she does not want a child, there are many who find it difficult to reach any firm conclusion. If a woman is doing well in her career and progressing up her chosen ladder, it is understandably difficult to decide to give it all up – albeit temporarily – to start a family. Will all the study and effort that she has put in to her job be wasted? Will she ever be able to re-enter her career at a comparable position or will she have forfeited her chances of advancement for ever? (Fortunately many more employers are now making sure that it is possible for women to take time off for pregnancy and childcare without losing status). And suppose she does decide that she wants to have a child; will she find it difficult, after being used to a busy lifestyle amidst adult company, to stay at home with her baby?

COMBINING CHILDREN WITH WORK

It seems that whatever decision a woman makes in such circumstances, she will end up feeling guilty. If she chooses to continue with her career and remain childless, she will be made to feel 'unfeminine' or 'unnatural'. If she takes time off to have her baby and to stay at home and look after it, she is 'wasting' her intelligence and her ability and letting down her company. If she has a child and then hires a nanny so that she can return to work, she is a bad mother who does not care for her baby. It is bad enough when other people (plus many elements of the media) conspire to create these feelings of guilt. It is far, far worse when the guilt comes, as it so often does, from within the woman herself.

Case Study: Danielle

Danielle had a position of considerable authority and responsibility with a large fashion house. She loved the work, even the long hours and the often unreasonable demands of the highly strung designers. A chic and elegant Frenchwoman, she had worked her way up within the fashion house, having begun by being given the lowliest of tasks when she joined them after leaving school in the suburbs of Paris, when she was just sixteen. At the age of thirty-four Danielle married a wealthy businessman some years her senior, a man who absolutely adored her. They lived a life of luxury with a big house in the country and apartments in both London and Paris.

Happy as she was with her career, Danielle had always known that she would one day wish to have children so she was delighted – as indeed was her husband – when she became pregnant just eight months after her marriage. It was an easy and healthy pregnancy and Danielle was able to work until a few weeks before the birth of her baby daughter. As she had always planned to do, she hired a nanny to look after the child and returned to work when the baby was just four weeks old.

Although Danielle loved her work as much as ever and knew that she would never have been happy staying at home and playing a purely domestic role, nonetheless she felt pangs of regret from time to time that she did not have as much contact with her little daughter as she would have liked. She no longer travelled as extensively as she had previously done and she always tried to be home early enough to spend some time with her baby before bedtime. But she had to admit to herself that it hurt her to think that someone else saw the first toothless smile, someone else heard the first spoken words and someone else reached out to steady the toddler as she took her first wobbly steps. Perhaps the most difficult moment came about two years later when, on a sunny Sunday afternoon in the garden, the little girl fell over and – completely ignoring her mother – ran straight to her nanny for comfort.

Case Study: Vanessa

Unlike Danielle, Vanessa had no desire for children of her own. She preferred to concentrate on her career as editor of a well-known glossy magazine. Brian, the man with whom she lived, had been married before and already had two adult sons, so he was not unduly perturbed at the thought of no more children. He and Vanessa enjoyed going to the theatre, eating in good restaurants and travelling widely in whatever time their respective careers allowed them to have together.

As Vanessa observed other women trying to juggle the responsibilities of career and family or having to give up work altogether in order to care for their children, she would feel somewhat smug about the decision she had made. As she went from her thirties to her forties she felt only the occasional pang of regret. By the time she reached forty-five she began to wonder from time to time whether she had come to the wrong conclusion all those years ago. When she went through her menopause her regret turned to bitterness as she contemplated opportunities now lost for ever. She blamed herself for what she saw as her selfishness. The glittering career now seemed to be tainted. She began to wonder what would happen when she retired or what she would do if Brian died before she did – which was quite possible as he was some years older than she was. They had been so busy with their respective careers and spending their precious spare time together that they had few real friends. Vanessa dreaded the thought of a lonely old age and now bitterly regretted her earlier decision.

Of course not everyone in Vanessa's position feels as she does. There are plenty of women who decide not to have children and who are perfectly content with that decision for the rest of their lives – particularly when their partner is caring and supportive. There are others who cannot envisage a life without children and go on to have a family without any regret. Stress and guilt only appear on the scene when the woman is not really at ease with the decision she has made or when she feels that she has been coerced into it by her partner, her family or some other external influence.

How could Danielle and Vanessa have reduced the amount of stress created by their own decisions? Once Danielle had made her choice and decided that, much as she loved her little daughter, she wanted (or needed) to return to work, she had to accept the fact that someone else would be playing a major role in her child's life. All she could do was to ask herself whether being there for every new stage in her baby's development was sufficient compensation for giving up a fulfilling career. As for Vanessa, having made her choice and eventually reaching the stage where it was impossible for her to have a child, there was nothing she could do to change the situation. The past slips out of our control but we still have some say about the future. If what she feared was a lonely old age, it was up to her to cultivate friendships long before such a time arose – and one can only acquire friends by being a friend to others. However dedicated one is to one's career or to a partner, it is always possible to find time and space in life for other people.

All the situations mentioned in this chapter are ones to which there is no 'correct' answer. In each case the decision must be made by the individual or the couple concerned. However, there are some important points to be taken into consideration.

* It is vital to weigh up the situation as thoroughly as possible before coming to any decision at all. Discuss the pros and cons with your partner. Think about the effect of your decision upon the future and decide on your long term hopes and desires.

* Once you have made your decision, there is much to be gained by reviewing the situation from time to time. What you want at thirty may not be the same as what you wanted at eighteen. There is nothing to say that you cannot change your mind, provided you do it through choice and not because you feel that you are being pressured to do so.

* If you reach a point of no return – as in the case of Margie and Dave when, having already moved into their larger house, conception proved so difficult, or when Vanessa reached her menopause, thus putting an end to any possibility of a child of her own – do not waste time regretting former decisions. Of course you should do what you can to make the best of the situation so far as the future is concerned but there is absolutely nothing you can do about what has already gone and anger or bitterness about the past can only increase the amount of stress you feel.

* Be sure that the decisions you make are your own or a willing compromise between you and your partner. Do not allow yourself to be influenced by what you read or hear or by

what others do – or indeed what other people think you should do.

* Remember that guilt, like anger, is a terrible waste of energy. Use that energy in a positive way instead and do what you can to improve the situation if at all possible.

* Take steps to deal with any tension you may feel so that you do not add to any problems you may have by suffering physically or mentally from stress-induced health conditions.

4

A Woman's Work . . .

Until now I have dealt mainly with the problems of stress in women who find themselves having to make decisions concerning their wish to pursue their own careers and their desire for a family. But, even when such problems do not exist and the woman has a satisfactory and fulfilling career in what was – and in many cases still is – thought of as a 'man's world', there are still stress-inducing factors to be dealt with. It is just that she has an entirely different set of problems facing her – and this applies whether she is attempting to return to work after a prolonged absence or whether she is one of those dedicated careerwomen who have never had any desire for the traditional home and family life.

A MAN'S WORLD

We are told that we live in an age of equal opportunity but is it? It is still the exception rather than the rule for a woman to reach top management level. In fact, the only way she can be *sure* of doing this is to start her own business – a situation which can sometimes lead to all the stresses and none of the perks! Running your own business – particularly if you start off in a small way as many people have to do – can mean that you are your own personal assistant, secretary and tea lady! However, more and more women are finding that this is the only way that they can reach the top, not because of any lack of ability

45

but because of the prejudice they encounter when working for some of our larger organisations. Perhaps this situation will eventually be different when today's younger executives reach the most senior levels; after all they are far more used to seeing women doing jobs of equal or greater importance than their own. The majority of the men who hold the most senior positions in larger companies at the present time began to climb the corporate ladder in an age when women did not compete for the positions they now hold and many of them – especially those who are older and more set in their ways – still tend to think of female employees as secretaries or, at the very most, personal assistants. It is no myth that a woman often has to work twice as hard as a man if she wishes to be taken seriously and to advance in her chosen career.

Case Study: Deborah

Deborah was thrilled when she heard that she had been appointed to the Board of Directors of a leading wine import company. It seemed as though all her hard work and effort had been worth while. Little did she realise that her problems were only just beginning and that she would find her new elevated position far more stressful than any she had encountered on the way. She had become an expert on her subject having studied all aspects of the wine trade and taken examinations to achieve all the necessary qualifications. She knew her job well and had worked as head of her department for some time before being elected to the board.

At the monthly board meeting each head of department would give a report on the previous month's results, answering questions and replying to suggestions put by other members if these arose. There would then be a general discussion on policy and financial matters when each member would be able to give an opinion which would be listened to with respect by the rest of the board. Each member, that is, except Deborah. Like all the others, she would give her monthly report. This was rarely the subject of criticism as her department was achieving more and producing better results than it had ever done before. And yet, apart from a formal acknowledgement, no one ever seemed to comment upon what she said. And when it came to general discussion, on the few occasions when Deborah was able to make a point she was acutely aware of the condescension on the faces of her colleagues. Indeed, as she once commented to me, she almost expected them to lean over and pat her on the head for being a good little girl. It was not that anyone was actually unpleasant to her; it was simply that they did not seem to be prepared to take her seriously or to listen to her opinion. As the youngest, as well as the sole female, member of the board, she did not feel that she could leap to her feet shouting 'Listen to me', but she found the situation increasingly intolerable. Not only did she begin to feel that she was losing confidence in herself as a worthwhile member of the board – after all, no one else seemed to think much of her – but she found that, as the time for the monthly meeting approached, she was beginning to suffer from headaches (something she had never experienced before) which were not caused, as they often are, by fear and anxiety but by a sense of frustration and mounting indignation. She began to sleep badly for the first time in her life and, because of the tiredness she then experienced, found that she was becoming irritable and impatient with both herself and her staff.

If you feel that you are trapped in a frustrating situation at work – even if your problem is not precisely the same as Deborah's – take some time to examine your options and consider the results of any possible course of action. When Deborah first consulted me we decided to look at all her choices.

1. *Did she want to stay in her present position or did she feel that she would be happier working for another company?* On this matter Deborah was quite certain of what she wanted. She did not wish to leave the company for many reasons: she felt that it would be admitting defeat and might even appear petulant were she to resign; she enjoyed her work as head of department and revelled in the challenges presented by the job; in spite of the difficulties she was experiencing, at least she had been appointed to the Board of Directors and it was unlikely that such a position would easily come her way in another company. So, having weighed up all the possibilities, she had no doubt in her mind that she would prefer to stay where she was.

2. *She could remain in her job and let things go on as they had before*. She could continue to do her work efficiently and well and then, when it came to the time for the monthly board meeting, she could simply give her report and then remain quiet, contributing nothing further to the proceedings. Deborah informed me immediately that such a situation would be intolerable. Not only would it make a complete mockery of all her efforts to date but she felt that she often had valid points to make and did not see why she should not have a chance to do so. In addition, because she had reached her present position at a comparatively young age, she knew that she would be likely to progress further up the business ladder – but she felt that this was not going to happen if she merely sat back and remained silent.

3. *Having come to the conclusion that something had to be done, Deborah then had to take time to weigh up the various possibilities which sprang to mind*. Should she approach the Chairman? She thought not as this elderly man obviously felt that he had already done more than enough by having a woman on the board in the first place. Should she approach one of the other board members? Deborah hesitated about taking this action as she did not want it to appear that she was being underhand or trying to play off one member against another.

Having sorted out in her own mind what she wanted to achieve and those methods which she felt she could *not* employ, Deborah then had to work out a plan of action – and this is what she did.

First of all, she spoke to the secretary and wrote a letter of confirmation, requesting that she be put on the agenda for the next meeting. This would mean that there would be a specific time when she would be able to make any points she wished.

For two weeks before the actual date of the meeting, she spent time each day counteracting any stress which might be building by practising a relaxation technique. In addition she rehearsed mentally for the forthcoming meeting – visualising the situation and imagining making her points and dealing with any difficulties which might arise without allowing her annoyance or irritability to show.

Naturally it was essential for Deborah to prepare well for the meeting. She had to check all her facts and then to have them at her fingertips. The other members of the board were by no means stupid and she knew that, provided her points were valid, they would listen. The difficulty until now had been finding an opportunity to make those points.

Although, as the time approached, Deborah naturally became a little apprehensive, she managed to keep this under control by asking herself one simple question, 'What is the worst that can happen?' She was not going to be demoted or to lose her job – she knew her department's excellent results would ensure that. The worst that could happen would be that no one would take any notice of what she was saying but this was extremely unlikely as the members of the board were all interested in improving and increasing the business and would not turn down any sensible idea. If the worst *did* happen and her points were ignored, she would simply be in the same position as before and would just have to consider a different strategy.

Deborah carried out her plan. At the meeting the following month she was able to make her points clearly and succinctly and, because she had all the information with her, she was able to answer any question put to her. Not only were some of her suggestions accepted but she felt that her credibility as a member of the board had increased dramatically and that the other members would be more likely to listen to anything she might have to say in the future.

Now, any difficulties you might encounter in the course of your working life are likely to be quite different from those that Deborah had to face. But the basic plan of action is the same. Consider the checklist below and see if you can adapt it to help you deal with any problems you may have.

Checklist

1.   Consider your options and rule out any action which is unacceptable to you.

2.   Make plans but do this in your own time and when you are not in the middle of a stressful situation.

3.   Unless haste is absolutely essential, allow yourself time to practise a relaxation technique to dispel any feelings of stress from which you might be suffering.

4.   Rehearse any scenes or confrontations in your mind so that you become familiar with them and nothing can take you by surprise.

5.   Prepare well. Have any relevant facts immediately to hand so that you do not let yourself down in front of others by lack of knowledge.

6.   Ask yourself, 'What is the worst that can happen?' If you can cope with the worst, anything else must be an improvement.

7.   Carry it through. All the thinking, imagining and planning in the world are to no avail if you never get to the point of doing anything about the situation.

SEXUAL HARASSMENT

It is an unfortunate but true fact that sexual harassment still exists at all levels in the working environment. And although some women are able to ignore or cope with the situation, many others find the whole problem most distressing. Sexual harassment, of course, can mean many different things, ranging from the telling of offensive 'jokes', through suggestive behaviour to what amounts to assault. Of course there are some women who take offence where none is intended and who are only too ready to read innuendo into the harmless remark or to construe a friendly touch on the arm as a sexual advance. But the fact remains that there are indeed many cases of sexual harassment towards women at their place of work.

Only recently there was the widely reported case of a woman train driver who was physically manhandled by another driver in a way which can only be described as indecent assault. When the victim complained to her superiors, it was *she* who was transferred to a position of lower status where she had less job satisfaction and less money. There have been several reported cases of secretaries whose bosses felt that they were paying for more than mere shorthand and typing skills. When these women tried to complain, they were either not believed or they were threatened with the loss of their jobs with no satisfactory reference. This put them in the intolerable position of having to stay where they were (and perhaps continue to put up with unwelcome advances) or find themselves out of work with no money and no immediate prospects.

Case Study: Ruth

Ruth is a freelance television presenter and has to travel extensively in her work. In fact, nearly one fifth of all

British business travellers are women and the number is growing year by year. And yet such women are often victims of discrimination and harassment in hotels.

Ruth's job frequently involves working unusual hours and she told me of a recent incident when she was staying in a large top grade hotel in a northern city and she had to call for a taxi in the early hours of the morning as she was appearing that day on breakfast television. Perhaps because her job called for her to be well dressed and made up, despite the early hour, she had to endure the humiliation of several 'knowing' remarks and comments as she crossed the reception area. Other women have told me that they spend most of their free time, when travelling on business, in their hotel bedrooms. Quite often the only lounge area is the bar and there are still men – usually those who want to show off before their colleagues – who feel it almost a duty to 'chat up' any single female. In addition, those women who dine alone in hotels are often treated less favourably than the men – given bad tables, inferior service and so on. Ruth said that she found hotels lonely and felt that she missed out on social life and camaraderie. She would have liked to sit and talk with others in the lounge or bar but such behaviour was always taken to be an invitation to something more.

This is by no means intended to be an indictment of all hotels. Indeed some of the larger chains now have a special policy for women guests who are travelling alone. It is not simply a case of the bedroom being equipped with such extras as hairdryers and make-up mirrors but also of offering peace of mind by having a peephole and security chain on the door and a special card to cover the key number. If you have to travel alone, it is well worth while enquiring whether your chosen hotel provides such facilities – after all, it is only when women insist on such amenities that more hotels will begin to offer them.

Case Study: Joanna

Motoring has its problems too. Joanna had been attending a three day seminar in a hotel in the north of England. She was driving back down the M6 at about 10pm one night when she saw in her rear view mirror that the car behind was flashing its lights repeatedly. At first she thought that perhaps something was wrong with her vehicle and she checked the dashboard for any warning lights but all seemed to be well. Suddenly she realised that she was being deliberately harassed. She drove a little faster – so did the car behind. She drove a little slower – so did the car behind. She changed lanes – so did the car behind.

Joanna could feel panic rising within her; she did not know what to do. Should she accelerate and try to get home as quickly as possible or should she slow down in the hope that the other vehicle would pass? Should she keep changing lanes and try to put him off? If she were to slow down or change lanes repeatedly, that might just make the other driver think that she was enjoying the 'game' and encourage him to continue. But she realised that to drive faster than usual – particularly when she was nervous – would be extremely dangerous.

I spoke to the head instructor of a company which runs, among other things, courses for women to help them deal with precisely this sort of situation. His advice was that you should slow down (but not stop) as this usually causes the other driver to become bored and to look for a new victim. Although one should not become paranoid and look for harassment everywhere, there are several common sense things which can be done to reduce the risk of it happening to you – and, if you reduce the risk, you reduce the stress you are likely to suffer.

* Do not leave anything in full view which immediately identifies you as a woman. Keep shoes, glossy magazines, and so on, out of sight.

* If you are out for the evening in a low cut dress, make sure that you wear a covering coat or jacket.

* Remove any swinging toys, 'cute' notices, and so on as it seems that these often imply a 'swinging' personality.

* If you cannot afford a real car phone, invest in one of the excellent imitation ones available. The thought that you might be telephoning for help will be enough to deter a persistent pest.

* Go on one of the courses intended to help you deal with just such a situation; you will feel much better if you know that you are in control.

* Don't panic! Although there are cases of women drivers being harassed in this way, it is really quite a rare occurrence.

RETURNING TO WORK

For many women, going back to work after a prolonged absence brings ts own problems and decisions – although it has to be said that in many cases more stress is caused by the *thought* of returning to work than by the reality of the situation when it arises. It is a sad fact that the lack of confidence associated with such stress-induced anxiety often results in many women accepting inferior posts or poorly paid, part time work rather than the positions to which their background and experience would entitle them.

Case Study: Angie

> Until the birth of her first child, Angie had worked as a secretary in the office of a thriving law practice. She had made a conscious decision to stay at home and look after her children until the youngest was at school all day. But how things had changed during those few years. Suddenly offices had become a high tech world of computers, word processors, fax machines, electronic equipment of all sorts – all things of which Angie had no knowledge or experience. How, she wondered, could she ever catch up with all that she had missed? Would she ever be able to cope with a secretarial job again?

It is because of the problems facing such women as Angie that several schemes exist which enable skills to be updated by training or retraining. Indeed, many of the larger organisations run their own programmes to help those women who have taken maternity and parental leave to keep abreast of those changes which have taken place. At least one of the major banks gives its female employees a 'career break' of anything from one to five years. During this time each woman has to return to work for just two weeks each year and to attend an annual one day seminar; she also receives regular newsletters giving her the latest information about the banking world in general and the specific organisation in particular.

Because of the help which is now widely available, there is no need for any woman to feel that she will not be able to cope or that she must take a part-time job or one which is beneath the level of her ability. In recent years so much talent has been allowed to go to waste because of the lack of confidence felt by many mothers contemplating returning to work; it was often easier to say that she would just take a 'little job' because her children needed her – even when those children were rapidly growing up.

If you are someone who is thinking seriously about returning to work but you feel that your self confidence is at a low ebb, there are many things you can do to build up your self assurance.

Courses

The types of courses available are many and can be fitted in to the majority of lifestyles. You can go to your local adult education classes (day or evening) for comparatively little cost. Some firms will allow you to start work at a slightly lower rate of pay but will train you in all forms of modern office technology. Specialised courses also exist which provide intensive training to allow you to acquire a specific skill. These are often quite expensive but, at the time of writing, it is sometimes possible to borrow up to 80 per cent of the cost as a Career Development Loan and you do not start to repay this money until you are qualified.

Job-sharing or part time work

This will often enable you to avoid a build-up of stress while acquiring the new skills you require. Because you only work for part of the day, or a few days a week, you have the opportunity to digest the knowledge you are acquiring in an easy and relaxed way.

Temping

This is frequently an ideal way of regaining your confidence and acquiring practical experience while earning. And, although we tend to think of 'temps' as secretaries and office staff, there are agencies dealing with every aspect of work from fashion stores to public relations, from computer programming to personnel.

Voluntary work

If your financial situation allows it, becoming a volunteer is an excellent way of regaining your self-confidence. Although it may not always be possible to work as a volunteer in the world of commerce, there are certainly many opportunities for anyone who is interested in social or therapy work and in these fields the greatest skills are acquired through experience rather than theoretical knowledge.

Start your own business

Because you can begin to do this in as small a way as you wish, you can allow your business to expand to keep pace with the increase in your feelings of confidence. Everyone has skills and talents and this is an excellent way to exploit them. It doesn't matter whether you start gradually in your spare time while doing another, more mundane, job or whether you prepare for running a full time business by building up slowly while you are still looking after a family; for many women there is little to compare with the satisfaction felt when working for yourself.

There is plenty of help about these days for anyone, man or woman, who wishes to establish a new business. If you are short of ideas, there are several books on the subject which will provide food for thought as well as give you information about the various rules and regulations, tax and accounting requirements and sources of financial help. Provided you meet the requirements, the Enterprise Allowance will provide you with a small weekly income for a year while you try to get your business on its feet and there are several government departments only too eager to help the budding entrepreneur.

So, let us suppose that you have decided to return to work. Where do you begin and what do you look for?

PLAN OF ACTION

1.   Take the matter seriously. Set aside some time, once or twice a week, to look for jobs (in newspapers or through agencies and so on) and to write letters.

2. Believe in yourself. Just because you have not worked outside the home for a few years does *not* mean that your brain has turned to jelly or that your former abilities have deserted you. Make a list of your skills, whether they are technical ones (such as typing) or personal (being a good communicator) and realise that each one of them has a real value.

3. Take a chance. Try applying for positions quite unlike any you have held in the past. You might find yourself entering a world which fascinates you – and you will certainly broaden your horizons.

The interview

So now the hoped for yet dreaded situation has arisen; someone actually wants to interview you for a job. Anyone, at any age, is bound to feel a certain amount of apprehension as the day draws nearer but it seems that no one becomes more stressed than a woman who has been away from work for a few years. Although no one can guarantee that you will succeed in obtaining a particular job – indeed, you may find when you get there that you do not even want it – there are certain things you can do to swing the odds in your favour.

1. *Do your homework.* Before the date of the interview, take the trouble to find out all you can about your potential employer. Telephone the company (anonymously if you like) and make a few enquiries – you can always say that you are working on a project or a thesis. And remember that details of all large organisations are to be found in your local reference library so you can look them up at your leisure. By doing your homework you will be able to ask all the right questions and make all the right comments at the interview itself.

2. *Visualise yourself being successful.* As soon as you know the date of the interview, spend ten or fifteen minutes each day sitting quietly and imagining the entire situation exactly as you would like it to be. See yourself in your imagination saying all the right things and behaving in precisely the right way with no obvious evidence of nervousness. All you are doing is what every actor does – rehearsing again and again so that you will give a perfect performance on the day. The fact that your rehearsal is taking place in your mind makes

no difference whatsoever. Of course this technique will not guarantee that you are offered a particular job if you are not a suitable applicant. What it will do is make sure that you do not let yourself down through 'nerves' – the cause of the downfall of most interviewees.

3. *Remember that first impressions count.* While you will want to appear smartly turned out, it is also important that you wear something in which you feel comfortable so, if you decide to buy a new outfit for the interview, wear it a few times first to ensure that you feel at ease in it. You are likely to be quite tense at the interview and this could cause you to feel warmer than usual, so take this fact into consideration when selecting your clothes. Whatever the position for which you are applying, it is best not to wear anything which is too startling or extreme – and do remember that this applies not only to your clothes but also to your hairstyle, your nails and your make up.

Caring for young children

You've done it! You've got a job and you are looking forward to returning to work. But what about the children, particularly if they are not old enough to go to school? Unless you are extremely lucky and have a fond aunt or a doting grandmother on whom you can rely, you are going to have to make arrangements for the care of your children. You have several choices:

Childminders When choosing a childminder it is essential that you ensure that the person concerned is registered with the local authority. And do go along and check on both the person and the place. If the childminder takes her job seriously, she will not mind this in the least. Look around. How many other children are there? What toys are in evidence? What food will be supplied? Never be afraid to ask questions and, if you are not completely satisfied with the answers, keep looking!

Nurseries Private nurseries can be quite expensive and, depending on the area in which you live, they may have lengthy waiting lists. There are also council nurseries, however, and these usually give priority to single parents or those with particular difficulties so, if you come into such a category, you may find that your child will be accepted into one of these.

Nannies This, of course, is the most expensive of all but does have the advantage of giving the mother far more peace of mind than any other form of care. After all, even an older child who is at school each day can be unwell and have to stay at home and this naturally causes problems for the working mother. Although a nanny is out of the price range of many people, for the well-paid professional woman it is often the ideal answer as it is for the woman for whom the fulfilment of working is of more importance than the financial reward.

If you decide to employ a nanny to care for your children, it is imperative that you insist on one who has the qualification NNEB (National Nursery Examination Board) or a recognised equivalent. Remember too that a nanny – who can live with you or come in on a daily basis – is unlikely to do any housework other than whatever might be involved in caring for the children.

Whatever choice you make, take your time. This is not a decision to be made in a hurry if you are to avoid the stress of wondering whether you have done the right thing for your children or the guilt if you think you have not. And, for the children's sake as well as your own, make sure that they are well aware (provided they are old enough) of the situation. You will cause them great insecurity if you tell them of your decision one day and disappear to work leaving them in a new situation the next. If they are too young to understand exactly what is happening, take the time to break them in to the new situation gradually before you leave them. Let them get to know the childminder, the nursery or the nanny while you are still around so that they realise that all is well and that this is just an extension of their mother's love rather than an alternative to it.

Playing the game

For any woman wishing to forge a career for herself in the business world things can still be quite difficult. Not only does she have to contend with long held beliefs (particularly among older businessmen) that the woman's role is always secondary to the man's – even in the corporate world – but she has to battle with those instincts which are natural to her in the everyday life and to learn new 'rules' so that she can play the business game. I am not suggesting that these rules are good or bad – only that if you wish to succeed in the business world you are going to have to adhere to them. If you find them completely alien to your nature, then perhaps you will only find success in a world other than that of big business.

Keep your emotions in check Women are far better than men at making friends. Men will have colleagues at work, chaps that they drink with, pals they play sport with or even acquaintances with whom they go to the opera. But very few men have the sort of friends to whom they can reveal their feelings, tell their troubles or share their sorrow and joys. Most women however, whatever type of life they lead, will have at least one or two close friends to whom they can talk about their innermost feelings. But what works in everyday life does not necessarily work in business life. If you begin to talk about problems at home or in your emotional life, those around you will suspect that you are weak or vulnerable and may not be up to the demands of the job. So think before you speak or act and save those revelations for your women friends.

Present the right image Women in general have a great tendency to put themselves down just as they often idealise others. This, of course, is another way of saying that women often have insufficient confidence in themselves. Now no one is suggesting that this state of affairs can be changed overnight but there are several things that you can do.

1. *Create the right physical image.* It is amazing how much more confident you feel when you know that you look the part. It is not frivolity to take time over your appearance; it really can help you to feel better about yourself.

2. *Assertiveness training.* There are several courses presently available in this field. (And remember that being assertive is nothing at all to do with being aggressive.) Such courses will encourage you to assess your strengths and correct your weaknesses and to stand on your own two feet and stride out for what you want.

3. *Be prepared.* Make sure that you always have all the facts at your fingertips. There is no place in the business world for the ditherer. You will feel much more confident when you have done your homework.

Business is business   A woman who, when dealing with friends and family, is often accustomed to putting the needs of people before all else, must get used to the harsh fact that in business these needs usually fall very far behind the importance of money and power. If the woman then shows by her attitude that she is shocked by these values, she is unlikely to progress within the company.

You have to compete   Women usually find it extremely difficult to compete. For generations our upbringing has emphasised the image of the soft, gentle female – although, of course, not all women fit into this category. This does not mean that you have to become a harridan who argues over every point or is willing to stab each colleague in the back to get what she wants, but you do have to find a balance between being over aggressive and being too accommodating. Most women do not enjoy being manipulative but success in the world of business is frequently about manipulation.

   I realise that in this section I have generalised and that there are obviously many different types of women just as there are many different types of men. It is nonetheless a fact that, for a woman to succeed in what is still the 'man's world' of business, she has to play by the existing rules. To do so will obviously go against the nature of many women – and this I understand – but, if that is your case, perhaps you should not be looking at a career involving the scaling of the corporate ladder but something more suited to your personality.

5

Tug Of Love

Although your attention has been drawn to many of the difficulties which can confront any woman who has to make those seemingly impossible decisions regarding the conflicts between career- relationship- marriage- home- children, there are, of course, many women who manage to combine quite happily the worlds of career and relationship, whether they choose to marry or to live with their partner.

PARTNERSHIP PRESSURES

In fact, if both the woman and her partner have careers which are important to them, this often goes a long way towards solving many problems almost before they arise. Each partner will understand the stresses and pressures which face the other. There is less likely to be friction when one or other has to work late or to stay away from home because of career commitments. And a man who is deeply involved in a career of his own is not so inclined to expect the traditional male/female roles within the home.

Case Study: Edward and Delia

Edward and Delia were each pursuing a similar career in the business world, although with different organisations. Indeed, it was through their work that they first met, as they frequently found themselves attending the same seminars and conferences. Although they had been attracted to each other from the very beginning, it was some time before they decided to live together. Being about ten years her senior, Edward in fact occupied a far more elevated position in his organisation than Delia did in hers but, because of all the problems he had encountered as he progressed in his own career, he was extremely understanding of Delia's situation. He was helpful and supportive to her in many ways.

The relationship worked remarkably well and they soon established an amicable routine. They shared whatever housework was not done by the cleaner they could afford to employ; whoever was home first would start to prepare the evening meal; they were even in agreement that they had no desire to have children. As time went by and Delia, too, rose in the ranks of her company, their lifestyle became extremely comfortable. They both enjoyed their work; they shared the same interests; there was enough money for luxuries such as outings to theatres and restaurants and holidays abroad; they created a beautiful and comfortable home. Delia found herself wondering just why it was that other people seemed to encounter so many problems.

One of the reasons for the success of this particular relationship was that the stresses which affected both Edward and Delia during the course of their work were counteracted by the situation at home. The contentment felt by each of them enabled them to cope well with the pressures of their careers – indeed to flourish in spite of them. Because of their mutual understanding, each one was quite content and able to amuse themselves when the other partner was not free and yet they found pleasure in shared experiences when they did have time together.

Idyllic as Edward and Delia's situation may sound, even in such 'perfect' relationships troubles can arise. And, when they do, it is amazing how even the most forward thinking of men will frequently revert to traditional ideas, often without even realising that he is doing so.

At a special meeting held in the managing director's office Edward learned that the company was moving, lock, stock and barrel, to the outskirts of a large city at the other end of the country. Naturally they wanted Edward to go with them. He was offered promotion, a generous increase in salary, even help with moving. In fact the company was prepared to buy Edward and Delia's house at the current market price as well as to pay all moving expenses which might arise. Edward was so excited that he could hardly wait to get home and tell Delia the good news. He was sure that she would be as delighted as he was. The managing director wanted his answer by the end of the week but Edward told him that he was positive that there was not going to be a problem.

Delia's reaction completely amazed Edward. Not only was she stunned, she was furious. She could not believe that Edward had all but agreed to the transfer without considering her and how she would feel about it. Not only did she not want to move to the far end of the country, she had a perfectly good job which she loved, where she was doing well and where she felt that her efforts were appreciated. Why should she toss it all aside and start again hundreds of miles away? But the thing which hurt her most was that none of this had occurred to Edward and he was presenting her with what was, in effect, a *fait accompli* rather than asking her to discuss the matter with him.

Edward was completely taken aback. In his excitement over his promotion and his future prospects it had never occurred to him that Delia would not be just as thrilled as he was. He had to admit that he had not even paused to give a thought to her career. Meaning to be kind, he then made matters far worse by telling her that, with his increase in salary, she no longer needed to work. For the first time in their relationship they had a real row, each hurling angry accusations at the other. Edward was hurt and angry that Delia was not thrilled for him. Delia was hurt and angry that Edward had not thought her career important enough to take into consideration.

They were faced, of course, with a problem to which there could be no ideal solution. There was no way in which both could be completely happy with the outcome. Although it would not happen in every case, the strain on their relationship was too great and they parted. Some people would have been able to reach a compromise but Edward and Delia found that they could not.

I first met Delia about a year after the break-up. She came to consult me as she was suffering greatly from stress. She could not sleep; she was often tearful; PMT, which had never been a problem, was now almost unbearable. She was also experiencing difficulties with her work and her relationship with her colleagues and this worried her greatly. She spent hours each week agonising over whether she had made the right decision a year earlier. Should she have abandoned her career and gone with Edward as he had wished? It was too late now to change her mind as she had heard that he was now seriously involved with someone else.

In cases like this there is no right or wrong solution and no one can make the decision for anyone else. Whatever you decide, once the point of no return is reached, it is vital for your own well-being that you make the best of the situation. Once a decision is made and once it has got to the stage where there can be no going back, it is essential that you learn to come to terms with it. Delia had been faced with an extremely difficult choice. She could see that Edward would have been foolish to turn down the opportunity offered to him but what should she have done? It was a real 'no win'situation. Had she accompanied him to the new area she might have caused herself a tremendous amount of stress and anxiety by regretting all that she had given up. By staying she had become unhappy over the break-up of the relationship, although at least she still had her career. She had done the only possible thing she could do – she had made a decision. Now she had to learn to come to terms with it and to realise that, even if you cannot change the circumstances which surround you, you *can* change yourself and how much you allow those circumstances to affect you.

NO TIME TO RELAX

Although the majority of women now work outside the home at some stage in their adult lives, it is a fact that those women also take most of the responsibility for the care of the home and family. Oh, a couple may go to the supermarket together once a week to buy food but if they run out of something between visits it is usually the woman who is to be found dashing out to the shops during her lunch hour. This means that, whether she has a humble job or a scintillating career, the woman often does not have any time during the day when she can relax and undo any harmful effects of stress in her life until she falls exhausted into her bed at night. Even then she will often be mentally planning the next day's meals or wondering whether little Jimmy's football shirt had been washed.

It is important to remember that, although 'stress' is often thought of as the big, bad threat, it is not necessarily harmful. A little stress can actually give you the adrenalin boost you need to help you find that extra verve and energy or to enable you to think on your feet when instant decisions are required. It is only harmful when there is no let-up. It is rather like locking your car and going away having left the headlights on. They will shine brightly for a while but there will come a point when their energy will begin to fade – and eventually both they and the car battery will give up altogether and will not work again until they are recharged.

It is this 'let-up' which the majority of women do not have, although it must be said that in many cases it is entirely their own fault! Too many women have grown up with the idea that, if they are not fully occupied all the time, they are being lazy – and this causes them to feel guilty which brings with it its own stress-related problems. Since all it need take is fifteen minutes devoted to real relaxation a day to ensure that the harmful effects of stress can be reduced, if not avoided altogether, I do not believe that there is any woman who *cannot* find the time to look after herself and her health in this way, even if it means getting up fifteen minutes earlier or going to bed fifteen minutes later. This applies just as much to those women who are at home bringing up a family as it does to those who have a full time job. If you have school age children, use some of the time when they are out of the house; if you have a baby, make use of the time when he or she is asleep. (Details of a simple relaxation routine will be given towards the end of this book).

Checklist

Here is a checklist of ways in which you can alleviate stress in yourself.

1. *Talk things over.* So many couples, once they have been together for a while, forget to talk about what matters to them but fill their conversations with trivialities. Now, no one wants to spend all their spare time discussing their deepest inner feelings

but it is all too easy to assume that the person with whom you have been sharing your life automatically understands how you think and what worries you. This is not fair to either of you. It could be that your partner is going through life happily oblivious that there is something in your relationship which disturbs you and which could easily be adjusted – if only you would tell him about it.

2. *Make plans.* If you are both working it is quite a good idea to construct some sort of rota so that you both realise from the outset just how the home tasks are to be divided between you. Naturally, each couple must decide upon the routine which suits them but you could include such things as: first one home prepares the evening meal, the other washes up afterwards. Or: the last one to use the bathroom is responsible for cleaning it (this has been known to turn many a man into an early riser!) You must adapt this idea to suit yourself and your own circumstances and, once it is made, try and stick to it as much as possible, although naturally allowing room for variation when circumstances demand it.

3. *Make sure you have a 'switch-off' time each day.* It is vital for your mental and physical health that you have some time each day when you can relax and let go of the accumulated pressures and stresses. This switch-off time does not have to involve a period of complete inactivity. It does not matter whether you want to sit with your feet up listening to *The Archers*, take the dog for a walk round the block, prick out plants in the greenhouse or listen to your favourite music on record. What does matter is that you indulge in some pastime which brings you enjoyment and relaxation.

4. *Take longer switch-off times too.* Allow yourself some time each week when you are free – and this does not mean free to catch up on your household chores! If you have children, let your partner take sole charge of them for an hour or two, and of course you must be willing to do the same for him. Regular breaks throughout the year are also a good idea, and this does not have to involve expensive foreign holidays. Just a couple of days pursuing a favourite hobby – or doing nothing in particular – can be a wonderful pick-me-up. It does not matter whether you spend those days at home or away, although many people find that they are unable to relax fully at home as they are always far too aware of all those tasks which need to be completed. Many of us have been brought up to think of a two week annual holiday

but many women find it extremely difficult to do nothing for such a long period. If this is true of you, then a couple of days would provide you with a good stepping stone.

5. *Learn to relax.* This is probably the best way to combat the harmful effects of stress, particularly if you are someone who finds it very difficult to relax during the course of the normal day. You could try using the technique given later in this book, you could follow a yoga routine or you could make use of one of the many excellent cassettes on the market. But, whatever method you choose, it is imperative that you practise it regularly. This is the only way in which you will derive any real benefit from your chosen method. You could even indulge yourself from time to time by visiting an aromatherapist and having a massage or trying one of the other forms of help available (of which more later).

COPING WITH A CRISIS

We have already seen how women today are faced with innumerable decisions with regard to motherhood: whether or not they should have children; when they should have them; whether they should give up work to take care of them or should hire professional help to assist them. . .and so on, and so on. . . . But, even when you begin to think that you (hopefully with the aid of your partner) have satisfactorily dealt with all these difficult choices, you can still find yourself faced with hitherto unexpected problems, and the way in which those problems are resolved can have a long lasting effect on both mother and child.

Case Study: Margot and Tom

Margot had a responsible position on the editorial staff of a national magazine while Tom, her husband, was one of the senior members of the design department of an internationally known electronics firm. They had been happily married for fifteen years and had two daughters of twelve and thirteen. Both Tom and Margot felt that they had satisfactorily weathered all the crises which had arisen during the early part of their married life and had reached a stage where their relationship was based on mutual liking and respect as well as on love.

They had decided at the outset that Margot's career was as important to her as Tom's was to him and so they had always employed someone to help with the housework as well as a nanny for the girls when they were younger. The latter was no longer necessary, however, as the two girls went to the same school and Mrs Mann, the housekeeper/cleaner they currently employed, was always at the house in the afternoons when they arrived home, staying there until one of the parents returned from work.

All went well until an epidemic of chicken-pox attacked the pupils at the school. Both girls contracted it, although one much more severely than the other. Suddenly Margot was faced with the problem of finding someone to be at home all day every day with her daughters. It was not like the school holidays when the girls would often go and visit friends or have them to the house. This time, not only were they at home all day but they were not feeling at all well and needed to be looked after. And all this just at a time when the magazine for which Margot worked was planning a complete face lift, placing an increased burden on all the staff, particularly those at senior level.

In desperation Margot telephoned her mother to see whether she would be able to help, only to find that Grandma was going to Canada two days later to visit her younger daughter and her family. She knew that she could ask friends to help for the occasional day but it would be some weeks before the girls were out of quarantine and able to go back to school. She contacted a professional nursing agency but, because of the epidemic, they had been snowed under with pleas for help and would not be able to send anyone until the following Monday and this was only Tuesday!

When Tom returned from work and she was able to discuss it with him, Margot was astounded that he simply assumed that she would be the one to stay at home with their daughters until professional help arrived. It did not even occur to him to suggest that they each take a couple of days off to be with the girls or even that *he* should be the one to take responsibility for the situation. Margot tried to point out to him that, not only did she have all the usual deadlines facing any monthly publication to contend with, but that the situation was even more difficult at that precise time because of the changes through which the magazine was going. Tom was adamant. Margot was the girls' mother; it was her job to be at home with them when they needed her.

Of course Margot had someone else to argue with apart from Tom – and that was herself! Although she realised that the girls were not desperately ill, were old enough to understand the situation and could be satisfactorily cared for by someone else, like the majority of mothers she felt guilty at the thought of leaving her 'babies' at a time when they needed her. It was this feeling of guilt which she was unable to suppress and which finally induced her to accept the fact that she would remain at home for the rest of the week until professional help arrived to take over on the following Monday. She spent the next four days trying to do as much work as possible at home and running up the most enormous telephone bills dealing with situations which arose in her office.

The stress from which Margot found herself suffering increased daily. After all, consider the causes for that stress.

* Although her daughters were only suffering from chicken-pox, she still felt a mother's natural anxiety.

* She had always been able to cope with the pressure of deadlines and so on, which face anyone on the editorial staff of a regular publication, but that pressure had recently increased greatly because of the enlargement and redesign of the magazine.

* She had spent a tense and aggravating day phoning around and trying to arrange help, only to find that none would be forthcoming until the following week.

* She had expected her husband to be helpful and supportive as usual Margot had been amazed and angry that he had simply dumped the problem in her lap.

* She could not help feeling guilty for even wanting to leave the girls in someone else's care while she went back to work.

* She felt just as guilty for letting down the other members of the editorial staff when she knew they really needed her.

* Although she was able to do a certain amount of work at home, nonetheless it was a difficult situation and she knew that she was not really pulling her weight.

Apart from the fact that the added stress caused Margot to suffer from various physical aches and pains and to become tense and irritable, the situation actually affected all the members of the family. Tom and Margot found themselves arguing over anything and everything rather than the real issues; Margot snapped at her daughters and then felt even more guilty for doing so; the girls themselves, already feeling low because of the chicken-pox, became even more dispirited when they heard their parents constantly bickering.

Eventually the crisis itself was over. The girls, having been looked after by a very capable, if very expensive, agency nurse, recovered and returned to school. The magazine had a successful relaunch and the situation in the editorial office returned to normal (or what passes for normal in a life filled with last minute decisions and deadlines); with the easing of the situation, Margot became more like her old self – on the surface at any rate – and the stress-induced symptoms receded.

Although everything seemed to be back to normal, however, it actually took several months before the relationship between Margot and Tom was back on its old footing. And, had they not enjoyed such a good relationship in the first place, it is possible that permanent damage would have been done. Normally a caring and sensitive man, Tom was oblivious of the fact that Margot still harboured any resentment about the way things had turned out; and, although she was still very aware of the anger and bitterness she felt, she could not actually bring herself to discuss the subject with her husband for some time. When she finally did, it was Tom's turn to be amazed; he had had no idea that Margot was still bothered about the matter in any way. Of course it was not the fact that she had been compelled to take four days away from the office at a particularly busy time that was preying on Margot's mind but the fact that Tom had been chauvinistic enough to automatically assume that she would do so.

Once they actually sat down and talked the matter through and reached an understanding about each other's feelings, Tom and Margot were able to put the situation behind them and to enjoy a good, solid, loving relationship once more. But it took them a few months to reach this stage and, had they not both been able to express their feelings clearly and had the relationship not been such a steady one in the first place, there could have been a much more disastrous ending.

Tom and Margot's problem was by no means unique. Any working mother could find herself in a similar situation – after all, any child can be ill or have an accident at any time. Not everyone has a caring friend or relative close at hand on whom they can call, and certainly many of us would not be in a position to afford agency help. How would you deal with the situation? Here are a few points to consider *before the problem arises.*

* Once you have a family, take the time to sit down and talk to your partner about what you would do if you were faced with a problem similar to that with which Tom and Margot had to deal. Naturally you will not be able to consider every possible eventuality, but you can do your best. And just talking about it will ensure that your partner does not simply *assume* that the burden will fall entirely on you.

* Think of ways in which the working partner (whether it is the man or the woman) can play a part in reducing the burden placed on the one who has to remain at home. Perhaps work can be taken to and from the office; perhaps goods can be delivered or telephone calls can be made.

* Arrange for the working partner to help with the housework, the cooking, the shopping or simply being with the child during evening or weekends.

* Make sure that the parent who is at home being full-time carer is given some time off – whether it is to do some work, to go for a walk, to meet a friend or simply to lie in a warm, relaxing bath.

Competition or differences in status can be a cause of stress for many couples. If the relationship is built upon solid ground, this should not be an insoluble problem. When it does cause friction however, the difficulties almost always arise when the woman is in a higher position or is earning more than the man – not the other way around. The most awkward situation is one in which both man and woman are working in the same field – indeed, this is why most major companies have a strict policy that they will not employ both husband and wife; but today, with so many couples living together rather than marrying, the company may not always realise what is happening.

There are still some men, particularly those who are older or who come from a cultural background where boys are always considered to be more important than girls, who find it extremely difficult to accept the fact that any woman should be in a more senior position or in receipt of a higher salary. This difficulty is, of course, increased when they happen to be involved with the woman concerned. Surveys show that such men often turn to alcohol or to infidelity to provide them with an increased, if false, sense of self-esteem. This is merely a symbol of their own insecurity but such feelings are not helped by certain women who seem to take a delight in emphasising their professional or financial status and in doing all that they can to make their partner feel small. Such women have often fought long and hard to get where they are but anyone who needs to emphasise this at the expense of another is merely indicating that she does not feel particularly secure in her position.

Case Study: Gail and Bob

When Gail first met Bob she was working as an assistant researcher at her local radio station, having worked her way up from office junior/tea girl when she first left school. Bob was an accountant and had just set up in practice for himself. After knowing each other for several months, during which time Gail had the chance to fill in for several of the programme presenters when they went on holiday, the couple decided to marry and a date was set for the wedding to take place on Gail's birthday towards the end of the year. In the meantime, however, Gail was given her own daily programme – a morning show featuring a combination of records and live telephone calls from listeners. At first Bob was delighted for her as this was the chance she had been longing for.

Although she was not known nationally, Gail naturally became something of a celebrity in her own district. She was called on at regular intervals to open fetes or present prizes, and she thoroughly enjoyed the publicity. Bob, however, grew more and more sullen, refusing even to talk to Gail about her job. She, for her part, was totally unable to understand this, as she had expected him to be as happy for her as she was to see the steady expansion of his business. It was not even as though her income was anything like his and he had often told her that he would hate to be what he called 'public property'.

Their relationship deteriorated rapidly until they even discussed cancelling the wedding arrangements. Then, one day, Gail could stand it no longer. She forced Bob to sit down and discuss the matter with her. Finally he admitted that he felt that her fame, limited though it was to their own district, gave him a sense of inferiority. He felt like an appendage to her, 'Mr Gail Chapman', as he called it.

When I first met Gail she was suffering from several signs of stress. She was torn between her love for Bob and her desire to be her own person. On the one hand she felt guilty because she thought that she was the one causing the rift in the relationship; on the other, she did not see why she should give up something for which she had worked hard and which she thoroughly enjoyed. In addition, she was worried about the future. She knew perfectly well that she might never progress further in the world of entertainment than a two-hour show on local radio; but what if the chance arose to appear on national radio – or even television? Would she be afraid to accept opportunities offered to her because Bob could not live with the fact that she was better known than he was?

Naturally I could not – and would not – tell Gail what to do or what decision to make. She was the only one who could take that responsibility. But what I did point out to her was that she had no need to feel guilty about anything. She had not deserted Bob, had not harmed him in any way. If he could not accept that she was a local celebrity, that was *his* problem and not hers. I also felt that it was vital that the situation was sorted out before the wedding took place as this sort of conflict was no basis for a happy marriage. And there was no point in sitting back and hoping for the situation to change of its own accord – that was what she had done so far and all it had done was to cause her even more stress. She must decide in her own mind what her priorities were and she must talk them over with her fiancé, calmly and quietly explaining how she felt and, equally calmly and quietly, listening to his views.

This particular story has a happy ending as, after they had talked it over, Bob was able to realise that his love for Gail was more important than any unwarranted feelings of inferiority and the wedding finally took place as arranged. Of course things could have turned out differently. If Bob and Gail had cared less for each other or had not been prepared to make efforts to reach an understanding, then the relationship might well have ended. But then, if they had not loved each other sufficiently to deal with the matter, perhaps that would have been just as well!

Talking is so important in any relationship but particularly between couples who profess to love each other. More stress is caused by what you *imagine* the other person is thinking or what you *fear* will happen in the future than by any actual fact but all too often people, and women in particular, try to pretend that a situation does not exist rather than bringing it out into the open and discussing it, whatever the results. Don't be one of those people!

6

Money, Money, Money

'Money makes the world go around' or so the song tells us. But
the notes of the song tend to sound rather flat when you are
trying to exist on supplementary benefit or to bring up a young
family on a low income. On the other hand it is also said that
'money is the root of all evil' but this is not necessarily true
either. It only happens when you allow money to be your
master so that your desire for it or the way in which you
handle it colours every aspect of your life. There are, however,
many reasons why money can – and does – cause stress in the
life of many people, particularly women, and just a few of these
are described below.

MANAGING THE MONEY

Have you heard the old joke where the woman says: 'My
husband is definitely the boss. He makes all the important
decisions, such as which government should be in power, what
our defence policy should be and whether so much should
be spent on putting men into space. I only make the minor
decisions – what we should eat, what we should wear and
whether we can afford a holiday this year'. Yes, I know it's
corny but there is more than a grain of truth behind that old
chestnut. A couple may come to a joint decision about how
the family income is to be apportioned but it is usually the
woman who has to deal with matters on a day-to-day basis.

And because most women like to appear to be good managers – as indeed many of them are – those who encounter difficulties often do not like to admit the fact and this of course can lead to a great deal of stress.

Case Study: Irene and Jeff

Irene and Jeff had been married for some years. He worked as foreman in a local factory while she stayed at home looking after their three young children. While Jeff's wage could not be considered over-generous, it was adequate for their needs although they were able to save very little. The couple had worked out a sensible plan and did all they could to stick to their budget. When Jeff received his wages, a certain amount would be set aside to pay the mortgage, then the household bills. . .and so on. They were even able to put by a small sum for 'enjoyment money' so that they could have an evening out every now and then or an inexpensive family holiday. The rest was given to Irene for the running of the home and in general she coped quite well.

Irene had never been particularly organised in the way she did things but she managed the finances adequately from week to week. Then, without warning, there came a time when, all in one week, her eldest child had a birthday and wanted several of his little friends to come to a party, the second child lost his school pullover and had to have another one, while the baby developed a head cold and needed not only a prescribed medicine but a bottle of cough mixture to soothe his irritated throat. Irene was suddenly faced with the need to provide all these 'extras' but, because she had always spent whatever she was given each week, she had no resources on which she could fall back. She did not want to ask Jeff for the extra money as he had already been critical in the past about her poor management.

As the days passed and the financial pressure mounted, Irene grew more and more stressed. She could not sleep at night but lay there wondering what she should do. She began to suffer from headaches and to grow irritable with the children – and then felt guilty because she knew quite well that the problem was not their fault. The children themselves were sensitive enough to know that all was not well, although they did not know what the problem was, and soon they too became distressed.

What was Irene to do? What could you do if you found yourself in a similar situation? There is always more than one solution but, in order to put an end to the stress, it is necessary to deal with the matter in the short term before going on to look at what can be done to put matters right in the long term and to prevent a recurrence of the problem.

Short term solution Irene explained the situation to Jeff, although she wisely left the discussion for an appropriately relaxed moment rather than facing him with it as he came through the door after the day's work. He was a little critical of her management of the family finances but not unkindly so and he was able to give her some extra money to help her deal with the immediate situation.

Long term solution Irene and Jeff sat down together to work out new ways of handling the weekly budget. It was agreed that she would make lists of what she needed rather than go on in her former somewhat haphazard fashion and that, having planned for the essentials, she would do her shopping once a week (apart, of course, from any unexpected necessities which might crop up). Irene decided to keep a simple account notebook so that she could see where all the money went and Jeff told her that, should she find that she really had not enough to manage satisfactorily, he would do his best to give her a little extra.

Case Study: Julie

Julie's situation was quite different. She had a good job which she thoroughly enjoyed and for which she received a more than adequate salary. Julie's problem was that she *loved* to go shopping. She was slim, dark and attractive and she had excellent taste in clothes – and also a passion for acquiring them! At one time her spending had been controlled by the amount of cash she had in her purse or the balance of her bank account. But then came the fateful day when she was issued with a credit card. It was essential for her as, during the course of a month, she would run up considerable business expenses for which her company would then reimburse her.

Now there is nothing wrong in having one or more credit cards provided they are used wisely. For many people in Julie's position who incur considerable business expenses when travelling or staying away from home, it means that they are able to pay the bills without having to use their own money. And, since reimbursement for such expenses usually takes place before the credit card statement is received, no interest has to be paid. They can also be extremely useful in cases of emergency, such as the breakdown of a car, when the cost of repair might come to an amount higher than that covered by the normal cheque guarantee card. The real difficulties arise when someone like Julie has a credit card in her possession. Suddenly she is in a position where she is able to indulge her every shopping whim. Of course she never intends to spend more than she can afford to repay but the fact remains that, whereas the majority of people would be very conscious of the size of the bill that they are running up, others – like Julie – really get carried away by their newfound spending power.

Julie knew that the interest rate charged by the credit card companies on amounts outstanding is often exorbitantly high but, when she received the first statement after a major spending spree, that interest was somewhere in the region of £12. She decided that this amount was small enough 'not to notice' and so she simply paid the minimum amount demanded by the company. As the months went by, not only did the basic amount she owed soar with frightening rapidity but so did the amount of interest and it seemed to take no time at all for Julie to reach her credit limit. She began to panic. Now that she was not allowed to use the card until she had paid some of the outstanding debt – and even on her salary she did not know how she was going to do that – how would she cope with company expenses? She did not know what to do and so she did nothing. Not wanting her employers to know just how foolish she had been, she did not mention the matter to them. Not being able to repay more than a tiny part of what she owed, she did not reply to letters and demands from the credit card company until finally she received one which threatened legal action.

The stress of the whole matter made Julie physically ill. She began to suffer from breathlessness and anxiety attacks. She felt unable to eat but started to drink and smoke more. Her temper and her work suffered but the problem still did not go away.

What was Julie to do? How could she even begin to put matters right?

Short-term solution   The first thing Julie had to do was to contact the credit card company and explain the situation. When I spoke recently to the district manager of one of the major companies, he told me that they are quite prepared to be helpful provided they know that the borrower is trying to put matters right. If they feel, however, that he or she is trying to evade the situation altogether or has no intention of even trying to set their account straight, their policy is *always* to proceed with legal action. When Julie did contact them and explain what had happened, the threat of legal proceedings was dropped provided she agreed to pay a regular monthly sum until the total was reduced considerably – and, of course, she was not to use her credit card in the meantime.

The other thing Julie did was to speak to her employer and explain what she had done and that, because of the credit card company's ruling, she was unable to use the card for her normal business expenses. The interview with her immediate superior was not a happy one but Julie herself felt so much better once she had brought the matter out into the open. Her employer was not unreasonable and, although displeased at Julie's foolishness, agreed to give her an amount each month to cover her business expenses until she had paid off her debt and was able to use her credit card once more.

Long-term solution   If you are like Julie and find it difficult to curb your spending habits, you would do far better not to have a credit card at all. If you have one, perhaps you should cut it up and throw it away – it might be safer and would certainly be preferable to finding yourself faced with legal proceedings brought by the company concerned.

If it is essential, for business or other reasons, for you to keep your credit card, don't just leave it in your purse or wallet where you can reach for it without having to pause and think. Put it in a special container, perhaps something like a sealed envelope, so that you have to stop and think before using it and cannot do so automatically.

Of course the consumer society in which we live can bring about feelings of dissatisfaction – and therefore stress – in many people. Look at what we all have to face in our daily lives.

* *Television soap operas depict unrealistically affluent lifestyles* where the fabulously wealthy heroes and heroines seem to spend their days changing from one glamorous outfit to another (not to mention one silk-sheeted bed to another!) while surrounded by a positive retinue of servants. Although we all know that such programmes were never intended to portray real life, nonetheless many people – and particularly those with a somewhat humdrum daily existence – find themselves wanting those things which they know are going to remain perpetually out of their reach.

* Advertisements on television or in the cinema can *persuade you that you really want all sorts of gadgets or luxuries* which would never otherwise have occurred to you – and for which you have no actual need. The same applies to all that junk mail that comes through every door each day offering us unbelievable bargains, glittering prizes or an abundance of money by means of loans.

* Society in general is becoming more and more money oriented and *success is often judged in terms of material possessions*. This can cause some people to become dissatisfied and resentful about their material status or may induce them to set unrealistic goals or to pursue unattainable desires. All that happens is that then they become disappointed in themselves when they fail and this of course causes a great deal of stress, as does the treadmill of working extremely hard for ridiculously long hours in order to achieve the desired financial position.

Case Study: Patty and John

Before she married John, Patty had a reasonably good job as a secretary/typist in a busy office in the town centre.

After their marriage it was decided between them that she should keep on working until such time as she had a child and then she would stay at home to take care of her family. And that is just what happened. After three years of marriage Patty found that she was pregnant. Having a healthy and relatively untroubled pregnancy, she continued to work until a month before the expected birth. Apart from the fact that she enjoyed her work and the company of the other people in the office, she was able in this way to fully equip a delightful nursery for her coming child.

Patty and her husband were fortunate in that John's earning capacity was such that he was well able to support the family and he gave his wife sufficient money for the housekeeping, the baby and to spend on herself. They were both quite happy with the situation.

Then she saw the shoes! They were beautiful, they were elegant – and they were *very* expensive! In her old working days Patty would simply have decided whether she could afford them or not and acted accordingly. But now the position was different. She was unsure of herself. She did not feel justified in spending so large a proportion of the money John gave her on such an indulgence. She knew that he would give her the money for the shoes if she were to tell him about them but she felt that asking in such a way would be demeaning. And so a stress-inducing problem was created in Patty's mind so that eventually it was not the pair of shoes which was important but the whole situation of how she should act. She knew that she would feel guilty if she used some of the regular allowance for the shoes but she also felt resentful that she could not have them without having to 'ask permission'.

Short-term solution Rather than allowing resentment to build up within her, perhaps Patty could mention the shoes to John and ask for them as a birthday or Christmas present. (She knew, of course, that he could afford them and that she would not be stretching his finances in an unreasonable way).

Long-term solution Many women find themselves in just such a position. Having been used to working and controlling their own finances, suddenly they have other responsibilities and they are inclined to feel that any money they have is not theirs to spend. The first essential, naturally, is to discuss the situation with your partner so that he understands precisely how you feel. If you are not working and are relying on money given to you, once that money is in your possession you must be allowed to use it as you wish without feeling guilty. Naturally this should not mean rushing to the shops and buying the latest fashions while skimping on household and family purchases. But, although you will have to stay within your self-imposed limits, you are entitled to buy what you wish. Some years ago I worked in the Royal Courts of Justice and more than one High Court Judge of the Family Division has stated that the woman contributes just as much as her husband to the household when she stays at home taking care of the family.

Case Study: Joanna

Joanna was a single parent with a school-aged son. She was by no means unintelligent but she had left school with no specific academic qualifications. This resulted in her having to accept part-time, low paid work, her wages being topped up by state benefit. She found it hard enough to exist from week to week but things became even more difficult when money was needed for a new blazer or school outings. She certainly could not afford to pay a baby sitter and this meant that her social life was virtually non-existent. The effect of this situation was that, as time went by, she became more and more depressed with life.

Short-term solution   Joanna should try to find inexpensive or even free ways to cheer herself up. It costs very little to meet a friend for a cup of coffee – and nothing at all to feed the ducks in the park or have a free facial at the cosmetic counter of a department store.

Long-term solution   She could try and find out about courses which might help her to obtain some qualifications, and therefore a better job. Such courses are often available at special low rates to those on state benefit or with a low income.
   Joanna could take up an inexpensive, or even free, hobby

– perhaps jogging, swimming at the local leisure centre, sketching, or joining a local daytime adult education class. Not only would such interests cost her very little, they would provide a means of coming into contact with other people – something which was lacking in her present life.

The problems illustrated by the case histories above are all too common but of course the solutions I have put forward are by no means the only ones available. I am sure that you can think of others for yourself. What I have tried to show is that very few problems are incapable of being solved – with a little bit of help if needed. What follows below is a seven stage plan which should help you to identify and deal with your own problem. See how you can adapt it to your own life.

SEVEN STAGE PLAN

1. *What is the problem?* When considering your answer to this question, don't just say 'money'. Do you earn enough to provide for yourself and any dependants you may have? Are you extravagant? Do you hate having to ask for money, even when you know it will be gladly given? Be specific.

2. *What are your options?* Consider both the short and long term possibilities. Remember that there is not only one correct answer in each case so write down every possible solution that you can think of, even if some of them seem a bit far fetched.

3. *Study your lists* Rule out anything which you feel strongly you do not want to do and see what you are left with. Perhaps it would be possible to combine two or more of your options. If you come to the conclusion that nothing on your list is feasible, perhaps you have made your original list of options unrealistic.

4. *Put your short term plan into action* Now!

5. *Make definite long term plans* Write down every single stage of your plan of campaign in order. Try to give yourself a target date by which you should have completed each stage – but do please be realistic. You will cause yourself far less stress by dealing with each step ahead of time than you will by always

feeling that you are putting yourself under pressure because the targets you have set yourself are impossibly demanding.

6. Put your long term plan into action   Work methodically through all the stages on your written list; you will be astonished at just how much satisfaction is to be gained as you cross off each item. Never be afraid to seek outside help, whether from friends, family or a professional.

7. Follow through   Keep checking on your progress. Look at your list and study the stages of your long term plan after one week, then one month, then three months, for as long as necessary. If you find that your plan is not working out, change it. Don't feel guilty if this happens (after all, even finding out what does not work is progress) but simply reconsider your options, make another plan and try again.

Good luck!

7

One Is One And All Alone

There are many different reasons why a woman might find herself on her own or alone with a child or children to bring up. Sometimes that situation can arise because the woman has chosen it; either she has deliberately never entered into a committed relationship or perhaps she has been the instigator of a divorce or separation. At other times the situation will have been forced upon her; perhaps she has been widowed or has been deserted by her partner. Whatever the reason for the way of life – even when it is the woman's own choice – there is likely to be a certain amount of additional stress to be faced.

FACING FEAR

Even if she has chosen to live alone and pursue her own career and interests and even if she is quite happy with her way of life, it would be an unusual woman who did not experience moments of fear or apprehension. Many women admit to feeling vulnerable in the physical sense, although such feelings do not necessarily play a large or dramatic role in their lives. Thoughts of the possibility of some sort of physical attack or confrontation may cross the mind of one woman waiting at the bus stop on a dark winter's evening, just as it may hasten the steps of another who has to walk through the street at night to the place where her car is parked. Such apprehensions do not have to dominate the very existence of these women but they are there nevertheless, hovering in the background.

Case Study: Alison

Alison is a freelance journalist who has chosen to live alone in an airy flat in north west London. Calm and competent in most situations, she told me that she often experiences a silent twinge of anxiety as she puts her key in the lock when she returns home late at night or after a few days away. Due to the nature of her work, she does not keep basic nine to five hours and has no regular appointments. Because of this, it often crosses her mind that, were she to have a fall inside the flat or to become ill, she could lie there for days and no one would know what had happened. If, for some reason, she were unable to get to the telephone, there would be no one to call an ambulance. If she just had 'flu and felt sorry for herself, there would be no one to cool her brow and make her refreshing drinks – or even just to hold her hand and say 'there, there'. Naturally such thoughts are not always with her or she would not choose to live alone in the way that she does. They do lurk somewhere in the background, tending to rear their ugly heads when she is feeling low or vulnerable.

Although of course it is not possible to avoid every eventuality, there are certain precautions you can take to minimise those fears if you are someone who lives alone. They do not guarantee that you will not encounter any of the problems mentioned but hopefully they will give you added peace of mind and inner security.

* *Take steps to safeguard your home* to the best of your ability. Perhaps you could fit an alarm system or at least one of those outside lights which come on automatically as soon as anyone steps within their range.

* If you are going to be coming home after dark you could *leave a couple of lights on inside the house or flat* to give the appearance that someone is at home. Electric time-switches are relatively inexpensive and would ensure that lights went on and off at pre-selected times during the day or night,

something which can be a great advantage if you have to be away from home for several days at a time.

* If, like Alison, you do not have places where you would be regularly expected and where your absence would be missed and enquiries made, perhaps you could *find a friend in a similar position*. You could then arrange to contact each other every day or every second day so that there would be someone who would know if you were unwell.

WHEN A RELATIONSHIP ENDS

Instances of divorce, separation or the break-up of a long term relationship are becoming more and more common with each passing year. Such situations naturally bring with them their own stresses for both partners but it is often the woman who tends to feel them most acutely. As well as the distress caused by the unhappy situation itself, there is an inevitable sense of having failed. No one likes to think of themselves as a failure and women seem to take such feelings to heart to a greater degree than men, perhaps because of generations of being brought up to think of themselves as 'good wives and mothers'.

Going through the trauma of a divorce or a separation is distressing enough but, of course, before that event actually takes place there must have been difficulties existing within the relationship which were stress-inducing in themselves. There may have been accusations, anger, stony silences or just the sad and gradual breakdown of what was once a happy partnership. You may have found yourself confronted by the devastating news that your trusted partner has been indulging in one or more extra-marital liaisons – or perhaps you have had to cope with the guilt of an affair of your own. Whatever the cause (or, more likely, causes) of the deterioration of the relationship, once you have decided to part you still have to go through the myriad of practical problems: dividing up what you have always considered to be joint property, dealing with the financial situation, deciding what to tell your friends and families, consultations with respective legal advisers and coping with the questions and the well-intentioned sympathy and advice of others.

It is amazing how many couples enter into the commitment of a permanent relationship so bedazzled by their emotions that they never actually discuss what each of them expects from the other. Perhaps more couples should spend some time trying to put into words their hopes and fears and agreeing to compromise where necessary before linking their lives together. In fact they are more likely to spend time discussing what colour they should paint the living room walls than what they would hope to give to and get from their relationship.

The situation is bad enough when a childless couple separates or divorces but at least in such circumstances each of them has the opportunity to start again. When there are children to take into consideration there are many more difficulties. Whichever parent has care of the children – and this is usually, although not inevitably, the woman – has not only the added responsibility and anxiety of bringing up a family alone but is also likely to feel resentful from time to time that the other partner is now 'free' while her freedom is dramatically curtailed. This does not mean that she does not love her children or want them to be with her but, at times when she is feeling anxious about money or tired after a hectic day, she is quite likely to translate that resentment into irritability and bad temper towards them.

Case Study: Valerie and Anthony

Valerie and Anthony had known each other since their schooldays. They had married when Anthony was twenty-two and his bride only nineteen. Although she had worked until the birth of their daughter, Valerie had been quite happy to stay at home after that time to take care of the little girl and later her baby brother. As the children grew older and went to school, Valerie had returned to work in a local shop but both she and her husband thought of the money she earned as funds for extras and luxuries rather than as contributing to the basic family income.

A few days after her thirty-fifth birthday, Valerie was absolutely devastated when Anthony confessed to her that he had fallen in love with someone else, a woman he had met in the course of his work. Lisa was just twenty-nine, a career woman with no desire for children of her own. He told Valerie that he wanted a divorce and added insult to injury by saying that, although still very fond of her, he felt the need to be with someone more stimulating – someone 'on his own wavelength' as he put it.

Apart from all the practical problems with which she

was faced, Valerie felt unloved and discarded. Although Anthony was quite generous financially towards her and the children, there was certainly a definite drop in their standard of living. This was made even more difficult by the fact that, when the children went to stay with Anthony and Lisa, they experienced a more luxurious lifestyle and were given expensive presents and taken on exciting outings – something Valerie was unable to do for them. Not only that but she was the one who had to play the role of the disciplinarian. 'After all', as she told me, 'it must be easy to be nice to them and spoil them every other weekend when you don't have the daily responsibility of bringing them up.' Of course the children were more difficult to handle when they came home from these visits and it seemed that no sooner had they settled down again to their daily routine the time for the next visit came around. Valerie found that she was becoming physically exhausted by the need to earn her living, cope with the children and deal with all the problems of day-to-day family life.

As is quite common in such cases, Valerie fluctuated between feelings of guilt and feelings of anger. Sometimes she would ask herself whether it was her fault that Anthony had grown tired of her and sought the company of someone else. And then she would worry that she was not able to provide the children with the material standard of life she would have wished. At other times she would be furious that Anthony had simply walked away from the situation and been free to set up another and far more affluent home with Lisa. She grew more and more resentful. She felt that she had given Anthony 'the best years of her life' and that she had been dumped when it suited him. Because of their way of life, most of their friends had been other couples of a similar age and Valerie now felt out of place as the only single person in the group. She acknowledged that, although it was the last thing on her mind at the time, there might well come a time when she would be interested in another relationship but she wondered who would be prepared to take on a woman with two young children.

Suppose you find yourself in a position similar to that which confronted Valerie, what can you do? Once events have reached a certain point there is not much to be done about the circumstances themselves – indeed, that is probably for the best. What you *can* control is the effect that those circumstances have upon you and your physical, mental and emotional health. Naturally it would be unrealistic to think that you could experience all the trauma of the breakdown of a marriage or a relationship without feeling both stressed and distressed but there are certainly methods for counteracting the stress and avoiding those unpleasant conditions which are often stress-related.

1. *Accept what has happened* I am sure that you will already have put in whatever effort you considered appropriate to try and save the situation but, once you have reached a stage of inevitability, you have to make the best of things. Looking back and going over past hurts and disappointments is only of value if there is something to be learned from the process. If you can say to yourself objectively that you would act differently in similar circumstances or if you have been able to glean valuable information about your own personality or the type of person with whom you are most likely to be compatible, then at least something worthwhile will have come out of an unhappy time in your life. Once that point is reached, however, there is nothing positive to be gained by going over and over the past in your mind. All you will do is torment yourself with thoughts of 'if only. . .' or 'what if. . .', thereby increasing both the pain and stress of the situation.

2. *Cope with the present* Your first priority must be to consider how you can best survive what will naturally be a distressing time in your life. There are many sources of outside help, from legal advisers to Citizens Advice Bureaux, so don't be afraid to ask for help. Talk to your friends – you are unlikely to be the first person to experience your particular set of circumstances. The last thing you should do is bottle up your feelings and, even if you feel that you do not want advice from your friends, it is a great help just to know that they are there and that they care. Whatever happens, try not to allow yourself to turn to tranquillizers and anti-depressants as, not only is their effect relatively short lived, but you could find yourself faced with the additional problem of addiction. If you feel that you need to take *something*, it is better by far to turn to one of the natural and non-addictive remedies available from your local health shop.

3. *Deal with the immediate future* Instead of torturing yourself with thoughts of what might have been, concentrate on deciding how you are going to cope with the immediate future. What will be your financial situation and is there anything you can do to improve it? If you need to work and you have a young family, what arrangements can you make to ensure that your children are well cared for when you are not at home? This is a time when you should be preparing for your future, and there is a great deal to be said for writing lists and committing your plans to paper; it certainly helps you to get things clear in your own mind at a period in your life when you feel that you have a million and one points to take into consideration. Whether or not you will be working, try and think of ways to fill your days during the initial period after the separation. Many a depression has been caused by a woman sitting alone when her children are at school, feeling useless and unwanted. Perhaps, if you have the time, you could join a daytime adult education class or do some voluntary work. Perhaps you could meet friends more often than was previously possible. I am sure you can think of your own ways of filling your time in a positive and pleasurable way.

4. *Think about the long term future* Although in the early stages you will not be able to make definite decisions about what you want in the more distant future, it is often quite helpful to turn your thoughts in this direction – even if those thoughts seem for the moment to be little more than daydreams. Once you have sorted out present practicalities, consider whether you have any ambitions which it might now be possible for you to fulfil. Would you like to train so that you can work in a different field? Do you think that you would like to move from your present home (it doesn't matter if that does not seem to be financially possible at the moment – you are just considering what would be your ideal)? You may well feel so bruised and scarred emotionally by what you have experienced that you are not prepared even to consider the possibility of another serious relationship but there will come a time when you will probably need to examine your true feelings about just such a step.

DEATH

If most people find it difficult to talk about divorce or separation, the situation is far worse when you come to the topic of death. It is not unusual to find that, just when she needs them most, friends of a widow seem to go out of their way to avoid her. This is not done through unkindness or lack of caring but usually through diffidence or embarrassment – people just do not know what to say to the newly bereaved. They may well be there in the first few days when numbness and a sense of disbelief are natures' way of protecting you from the reality of the situation but, once that numbness wears off and you really need the warmth of other people around you, all too often they seem to avoid you. Sometimes this is in the genuine belief that you will want to be alone with your grief or that you will find it too distressing to talk about the one who has died whereas, in fact, the reverse is often the truth.

The woman who is to be divorced or separated has one advantage – she knows it is coming! In many instances the widow has no knowledge of the events which are going to overtake her. Of course there are instances where the woman and her partner are both aware of the impending situation and, although some couples find that this knowledge is helpful and enables them to grow closer to each other, the fact that someone you care for is approaching death can create its own sense of stress.

There are many stages to grief and ideally you should allow yourself time to experience them all. Naturally you will feel sad, both for the cutting short of your partner's life but also for yourself and the fact that you have been deprived of a future of love and closeness. As one woman, the mother of teenage children, said to me after the sudden death of her much loved husband, 'The thing which really hurts is that I do not come *first* to anyone now.' As well as sadness, you are going to experience any or all of the following: loneliness, numbness, fear, a sense of isolation and helplessness. There are two other emotions of which women often feel ashamed, although they are, in fact, a perfectly normal part of the grieving process – and those are guilt and anger.

Feeling angry and guilty

It may seem foolish or even unnatural to feel anger towards the person who has died and to blame them for leaving you to cope on your own. It may seem even more foolish to be angry with the world for continuing to turn, with other couples for growing old together or even with the sun for shining. But these feelings are quite normal and are experienced – although not necessarily admitted – by all those who grieve. And they will pass as time goes by.

Almost everyone experiences a sense of guilt after the death of a loved one. Guilt because of things said or done; guilt because of things *not* said or done or guilt because there was nothing which could be done. These feelings are increased when the bereaved person was not able to be there at the moment of death or was not able to go to the funeral. Although guilt is felt by most people, it always seems to be experienced to a greater degree by women. But then, women are the champions at feeling guilty in any circumstances.

The importance of crying

Never be afraid to cry. It is an essential part of the healing process after bereavement. 'Coping wonderfully well' or controlling your emotions has little merit and can do you untold harm – the British 'stiff upper lip' has a great deal to answer for! If you find that you are worried about crying in front of other people because you think that they will be embarrassed, tell them in advance that this is likely to happen and that you know that there is nothing they can really say to make you feel better but that there is a great deal of comfort to be gained when someone just holds your hand.

Talking about the one you have lost is excellent therapy in itself. This is not a morbid occupation as, in fact, you are unlikely to want to talk about the sadness of their passing. You are far more likely to want to talk about happy memories or amusing incidents in your life together and, although other people find this strange at first, they should be encouraged to talk too.

Initially it is very hard to be told that 'time heals'. It does, of course, but in the beginning you do not even want to be healed. You need time to think about what has happened and about the person who is no longer with you. Radio presenter David Jacobs is quoted as saying after the death of his wife, 'You never get over it but you do get used to it' and that is true. Time does make things easier to bear, although the amount of time the grieving process takes varies considerably from person to person. But, whatever your beliefs, you can take comfort from the fact that the one who has died is no longer suffering in any way at all. If you believe that human death is final and that there is nothing beyond, then the person is certainly in no position to suffer now. If you believe that there is some sort of life after this one, however you perceive it to be, then, once again, the person who has reached such a life is not capable of human suffering as we understand it. So really the crying is for ourselves, for our pain and for our loss – but that does not make it any less necessary if we are to experience all the natural stages of grief.

Great psychological stress is caused when the partner (or indeed any loved one) dies unexpectedly or as the result of violence. In addition to all the emotions already mentioned you are likely to experience a greater sense of anger plus feelings of shock and injustice, especially if the one who died was still young. In such cases you might benefit from talking to a bereavement counsellor or other caring professional (for details, see the end of this book).

Time heals

Although it is initially difficult to believe, the time will come when you are able to laugh again – and that time will be sooner than you think. There is no 'correct' grieving time as each person reacts differently. The first year is always difficult as you have to face every anniversary for the first time – his birthday, Valentine's Day, Christmas, Father's Day, your anniversary. . .and so on. But, although you will still be aware of these occasions the following year, once you have lived through them once it is far easier to do so for a second time. There will also come a time when you realise that days have passed without you thinking of him. Never let yourself feel guilty about this; it is perfectly natural and normal. After all, we are all likely to suffer the death of several people for whom we care during the course of our lives and daily existence would be unbearable if we were to spend all our time thinking of those we had lost.

Even when you think that you have finished grieving, there will be the odd occasion when you will suddenly be struck by all that you have lost. Some two years after my own husband died – at a time when I thought my grieving period was over – I knew that I was able to go to 'our' places, listen to 'our' songs or watch 'our' favourite films with no great sense of pain. But one day I was travelling on an underground train in London when a man came and sat next to me who happened to be wearing my husband's favourite after-shave. As the aroma drifted towards me I was aware of a sensation of grief and pain. The feelings passed after a few moments but they took me by surprise as until then I had considered myself to be 'over' my loss. But the unexpected can always catch you out.

How will you know when you are beginning to heal? When you are able to remember the good without it being over-shadowed by the sad; perhaps when you are able to pack up his clothes and give them to·charity or dispose of them in some other way; when you do not feel that you *have* to go to the cemetery every single week. All these are natural pointers to the healing process, and each of them is an important and significant stage.

If you still have children at home when your husband or partner dies, you can find yourself faced with additional practical problems of how to care for them both physically and financially and how to help them through the bereavement. However, those same children can also be your lifeline because you still have others around who need you and for whom you must care.

Death brings so much stress in its wake that it would be foolish of me to suggest here that there is much that can be done to alleviate your immediate problems. Nature is kind, however, and provides a sort of numbness which helps to carry you through. It is later, when you think you are 'over it', that you are more likely to suffer from stress. That is the time you need to take extra care of yourself, perhaps using one or more of the techniques described in the final chapter of this book.

FACING PRACTICALITIES

Whether you are alone by chance or by design and whether that situation came about suddenly or gradually, you will still find yourself faced with many of the same practical problems, particularly if you have children. You will need to work, whether for money or in some voluntary capacity depending on your financial state, and this has to be fitted in with the children's routine.

It is very easy at such a time in your life to forget yourself and your own needs altogether and this is the last thing you should do. You deserve attention too, so pamper yourself a little. This does not have to be an expensive exercise – a long, luxurious bath at the end of the day can give you time to unwind and can work wonders for you.

As with any other stressful situation, finding yourself alone again is unlikely to do you any permanent harm as long as you do something to counteract the build up of tension. The most generous gifts you can give yourself are time and consideration. Ensuring that you have some time to devote to yourself may take some skilful manoeuvring on your part but it is worth making the effort.

If you find yourself on your own again after having shared your life with someone, there are several things you can do to help yourself deal with the situation with the minimum of stress. Here are a few reminders.

The Past

Looking back is all very well but not if you indulge in it as some form of self-torture. If you genuinely feel that you have made mistakes, then learn from them by all means but do not open old wounds for the masochistic pleasure of watching them bleed. You cannot change what has gone but only the way in which it affects you and those around you.

The Present

Be as positive as you can. Remember that you need the company of other adults – babies may be delightful but their conversation is somewhat limited. Do what you can to meet other people, whether through work or social contact. Try not to shun your friends when they reach out to help; if you do that, they may not be there when you need them. Deal with your present financial position, with professional help if necessary. If you find that you have trouble sleeping, try drinking chamomile tea or hot chocolate before going to bed; whatever you do, avoid becoming dependent on pills or tablets. Give yourself time to relax and pamper yourself in small ways whenever possible.

The Future

Once you are over the immediate parting, however it came about, try and make short and long term plans for the future.

With regard to the long term plans, it is as well to remain relatively flexible as these may change as time goes by.

Being alone because you choose to can be an exciting and stimulating experience. If circumstances have forced the situation upon you, it is up to you to do what you can to help yourself. Give yourself a chance and you will be amazed at how much you can achieve.

8

It's That Time Again!

Women, of course are subject to all the stress-inducing factors which face men with one very significant 'extra'. It has been proved beyond doubt that, although it would be foolish to suggest that stress is the sole cause of all instances of pre-menstrual syndrome, period pains or exceptionally heavy periods, nevertheless excessive stress can certainly exacerbate existing problems and in some cases actually instigate them. This being so, those methods which are suitable for the relief of stress can also reduce the pain, tension and discomfort experienced by so many women month after month.

PERIOD PAIN

There are two basic types of period pain.
1. The first is not unlike labour pains in sensation, involving severe cramp in the lower abdomen. This normally starts with the onset of the period itself and can last for up to a week. All women react differently to this condition. Some, although obviously below par, manage to cope reasonably well whereas others feel so bad because of the pain that they have to take to their beds for prolonged periods of time. Some become nauseous or experience severe headaches while others become dizzy or faint. This pain is perhaps the one most easily counteracted by following a course of relaxation exercises.

2. The second type of pain begins well before the onset of the period itself. The woman will be aware of aches and pains for some days beforehand. She may find that her bra or the waistband of her skirt feels too tight. Perhaps she feels bloated; in many cases she will be aware of headaches or backaches. She may be irritable of short tempered and will even be more accident prone at this time. These symptoms can begin up to a week before the period itself but will usually disappear when it starts. Although the condition is different to the first one described, relaxation can help in this case too.

Why does something as basic as a simple relaxation routine help overcome what are primarily physical manifestations? When we are in pain we automatically tense the muscles of our body so perhaps it is easiest to consider first just what happens when we become tense. As you tighten your muscles through tension, various physical changes take place in your body:

*   your body produces an additional supply of adrenalin;
*   your heart rate increases;
*   there is an increase in your blood sugar level;
*   your blood pressure goes up to provide additional oxygen;
*   you begin to sweat.

Now look at what happens when you are able to relax:

*   less oxygen is needed so your blood pressure goes down;
*   your pulse and heart rate become slower;
*   you breathe more easily so you stop sweating;
*   your body stops producing extra adrenalin.

The last item is particularly significant as, when the body is producing additional adrenalin, it makes less of the hormones oestrogen and progesterone. It is a lack of these hormones which plays a large part in causing one or other of the types of pain described.

As soon as the human body experiences pain, it is a natural reaction to tense the muscles. But it is also a fact that the more you tense your muscles, the more you experience pain – so you simply set yourself on an unhappy treadmill which can last for days each month. However the reverse is also true: muscles which are relaxed experience less pain and therefore, because there is less pain, there is less need to tense the muscles.

How are you going to relax at a time when you are feeling tense and uncomfortable?. Try using any of the methods given in the final chapter of this book but do remember one thing. Although an initial stage of the relaxation technique requires you to tense and relax each set of muscles in turn, when it comes to any part of your body where you are experiencing actual physical pain, you should not tense them so much that you increase this pain. It is better simply to focus your attention on the area concerned.

As well as general pain and discomfort, there are certain specific problems which accompany the monthly period.

Vomiting

Sensations of pain and nausea are bad enough but the situation is made far worse if you know that you are usually sick too. Most people dread and fear that this will happen. Fear creates tension and if you are tense you are far more likely to be sick, so you are caught up in a vicious and unpleasant circle. There are, however, various things you can do to try and counteract these feelings.

* Practise a relaxation exercise regularly, especially one which involves the type of slow, steady breathing you are usually told to do when coming round from a general anaesthetic.

* Try and keep to a fairly light diet at this time. You will probably find that you feel better if you eat little and often rather than trying to have one large meal. Whenever possible, give yourself time to relax after eating.

* While the sensation lasts, try to avoid fats, alcohol and excess sugar.

* Try the old remedy of starting each day with a cup of hot, weak tea and a dry crispbread (not very nice but quite effective!).

Feeling faint

Some women just experience a sensation of dizziness while others actually pass out. As the skin colour of someone who is about to faint changes quite dramatically, usually becoming pale with a greenish tinge, others may be aware of the problem before you are and can warn you so that you have time to do something about it. Dizziness and fainting spells are less likely to occur if you have reduced your stress factor prior to the onset of your period. What else can you do?

* Remember what you were taught at school: sit with your head between your knees. When you feel better, don't be in too much of a hurry to get up but stay where you are and breathe slowly and steadily for several minutes.

* If you are in a crowded or inconvenient place, try clenching and unclenching your fists as quickly as you can while you make for the fresh air or for a handy chair.

* If you do faint, make sure that you do not start to rush about as soon as you come round, or it will only happen again. Sit still for a while and concentrate on your breathing.

Constipation

As well as the miseries of constipation, you are likely to find that your entire abdomen feels swollen and uncomfortable. Here are a few preventions and cures.

* Keep to the same light diet as that recommended for women who suffer from nausea. Make sure that you have as much fruit and vegetables (preferably raw) as possible. Start this diet about a week before your period is due if you know that constipation is a likely symptom for you.

* You may find it helpful to have extra fibre in your diet, particularly at the start of the day. Perhaps your breakfast could include wholemeal toast or cereal.

* Drink a cup of warm boiled water first thing in the morning – before you get up if you can find someone to bring it to you.

* Relax for as long as possible after each meal.

* Increase your daily intake of fluid.

Water retention

This is probably one of the most common discomforts encountered by women during the time of their period. It can begin to be felt several days before the period itself is due to start, although this varies from woman to woman. You can always tell when you are beginning to retain fluid as your bras, skirts, and so on begin to feel tight. You may find that you cannot put on or take off rings because your fingers have become swollen or that your ankles thicken and your shoes feel tight and uncomfortable. A woman's weight can go up at this time by anything from one to seven pounds, depending on the amount of water she retains in her body. Your breasts may well feel sore and tender. In addition, if you are normally susceptible to sinus trouble, the situation is likely to be worse at this time. What can you do?

* Cut down your fluid intake as much as possible. Do not do this to such a point that you are aware of being really thirsty but perhaps you could be more cautious about all those 'social' drinks – the cups of coffee with friends or the drink of tea because it happens to be four o'clock and so on.

* You can use diuretics but should do so with caution. Doctors will only prescribe them in severe cases and these should always be taken with medical supervision as they can cause you to lose a great deal of potassium from your body and you would need to take other tablets to replace this. Herbal diuretics, available from many health shops, are gentle but they are less effective and only seem to work for some people.

Changes of mood

These mood changes can vary from slight nuances to what amounts to a complete character metamorphosis. And unfortunately the changes always seem to be of a negative nature. You may become tense, irritable, depressed and either so full of energy that you find it almost impossible to sit still or completely listless and unable to function. You can, however, help yourself to some extent.

* If you find that you have an excess of energy, use it in a positive and useful way, perhaps gardening, decorating or

turning out cupboards. In this way you are less likely to become short-tempered and irritable.

* Before the date when your period is due to start, begin a course of regular breathing and relaxation sessions.

* Deliberately set out to do something which you find pleasurable. Life does not have to stop just because you have a period.

Fatigue

Fatigue only affects some women and it usually begins before the period itself. You may find that you feel tired when you wake up and that feeling remains with you throughout the day. Even simple tasks like making the bed seem to be an effort.

* Don't do more than you have to at this time; you can always make up for it later when you feel more like your usual self and have regained your energy.

* Take extra rest if you can and try to find ways of spoiling or indulging yourself.

* Make sure your diet is adequate. When you are feeling tired it is the easiest thing in the world to reach for the nearest available food rather than make the effort of cooking something nutritious – and that food is quite likely to be cake or biscuits. Take extra care over your diet at this time and see that you have plenty of protein-rich foods.

Even if you conscientiously follow all the hints given above and spend an appropriate amount of time practising relaxation and breathing techniques, no one can guarantee that you will sail through each month without the slightest sensation of discomfort. What you can be sure of, however, is that you will keep that discomfort to a minimum – and the lucky ones may banish it altogether.

9

Who Cares?

At the time of writing there are thought to be at least six million non-professional carers in Britain alone. These are people – and about 75 per cent of them are women – who have decided to devote a large proportion of their lives to looking after someone they love, or someone to whom they feel a duty. That someone is most likely to be a parent, a child or a spouse and their need for a carer may arise because of age, infirmity, disability or some chronic medical condition. The devotion of these carers has often necessitated them giving up a great deal, if not all, of their own social and working life.

But who cares for the carers? Who helps them to deal with the mental, physical and financial problems brought about by their labour of love? For caring is frequently a twenty-four hour job and, even when this is not the case, it is more than likely that it will be a twenty-four hour worry. Being a carer can mean that you are a virtual prisoner in your own home, often giving up your job, your independence and your social life in order to devote your life to someone who, in many cases, does not begin to appreciate all that you are doing – although often this is because they are simply not capable of understanding.

WHAT CARING ENTAILS

Caring is not merely an expression of love and devotion – it is also hard physical labour! Daily tasks often include lifting, carrying, feeding and attending to the toilet of the person they are looking after – and that person may well be unable to co-operate, thus making the strain on the carer even greater. The carer will also be faced with extra fetching, carrying, cooking and washing and may even have to put up with temper tantrums, abuse and frequent changes of mood brought about by the frustration of the patient. And, if that patient happens to be incontinent, the burden is of necessity even heavier. The carer will then have also to cope with daily changes and washing of bedding and clothing with all the physical effort this entails. In addition she may be called on to administer semi-medical therapy, such as assisting in the clearing of lungs, giving injections, helping with physiotherapy and so on. Although professional medical home help is available, a shortage of trained experts means that such resources as this may be limited and only available at certain times – and the rest of the time it is left to the carer to do what she can.

The carers I spoke to ranged from a young mother with a severely handicapped child to a woman in her late sixties looking after her mother who is ninety-four. Without exception, the thing they all claimed to find most difficult was the feeling of being trapped within four walls and the sense that they were being left to perform their duties alone, without physical or emotional support. Not one of them would dream of changing the life they had chosen for themselves as this would mean the person for whom they were caring would be forced to enter an institution. They just wished that they had some sort of moral back up, particularly at times when they themselves felt at the end of their tether. Some claimed that their doctors were extremely helpful while others felt that they were not given sufficient information about the types of physical and financial assistance available and certainly very little in the way of moral support. (Names and addresses of helpful organisations appear at the end of this book).

Case Study: Cheryl

Cheryl is the mother of two sons; Mark is a healthy eighteen year old while Joey is a severely handicapped boy of thirteen. He is about the size of a small eight year old and is unable to stand or even to sit unaided. He was severely brain-damaged at birth, leaving him partially blind and almost deaf. He is never going to get any better. Cheryl has been caring for Joey single-handedly since his father walked out when the boy was under a year old. Even at the most stressful times, she has never regretted her decision to do so as the only alternative would have been to put Joey into an institution and she had not been able to bear the thought of such an action. She did, however, feel extremely guilty about Mark. The boy had been only five when his brother was born and yet, since that time, Cheryl had been forced to give Joey constant attention. She felt that she had not been what she called 'a proper mother' to Mark and that he had been deprived of many of the treats and outings as well as much of the care and affection which other children take for granted. (I must say here that I met Mark on more than one occasion and he seemed to me to be a remarkably well balanced and composed young man. He had done well at school and was soon to go to university and he appeared to feel no resentment towards his younger brother).

Cheryl has more than Joey's physical handicap to deal with. The boy is hyperactive, rarely sleeping for more than a couple of hours at a time – and of course this means that Cheryl herself has not had a complete night's sleep since he was born. He also suffers from panic attacks and temper tantrums, brought about by his own frustrations and by his inability to understand what is happening around him. These tantrums are likely to occur even if Cheryl simply leaves him in the care of someone else for an hour while she makes her weekly trip to the local supermarket. A physiotherapist calls three times a week to try and keep the child's body relatively mobile and between those visits Mark and his mother do the best they can to carry out the same exercise routines.

Guilt and anxiety fill Cheryl's waking thoughts and torment her with bad dreams at night. She feels that Mark has been deprived of his childhood as she has had to rely on him so much – but how will she cope when he goes to university? And suppose she herself were to become ill, or even to die; who would take care of Joey then? She is permanently exhausted and sometimes feels that she can no longer go on. 'Is this all there is?' she wonders, and then she feels guilty because she is thinking about herself. She yearns for adult conversation; if only she could get out, even if it were just to go to the hairdresser or attend an evening class.

It is not part of my task here to question whether Cheryl was right to choose the life that she did. Mercifully I have never been put in the position of having to make such a decision and, even among those who have, there will be different ideas of the rights and wrongs of the situation. Cheryl took what she thought was the best path and, based upon that decision, let us look at how she can be helped or even help herself.

Obviously there is no way in which Cheryl is going to be able to change the basic pattern of her life but there are several things she can do – or which you can do, should you find yourself in a similar position – to make things a little easier for herself and to reduce the stress of the situation.

Short breaks These are essential for the mental and emotional well being of the carer. And it is not selfish to consider your own needs. Apart from the fact that you deserve such consideration, you will be far more able to cope efficiently and well with the situation which surrounds you if you feel that it is possible for you to have periods of relief. Perhaps Cheryl could help Joey to get used to a particular helper so that he would not be too upset if she were to leave the house for a while – even if, in the beginning, she merely had time for a ten minute walk. This could be gradually increased until she was able to take, say, an hour a day or a couple of hours in the evening.

Longer breaks If the patient is suffering from a specific illness, such as multiple sclerosis, then the association connected with that condition may well be able to help with information about special holidays, relief carers, and so on. In other cases, hospitals will sometimes agree to admit patients for a week or two to allow the full time carer to take a break, either so that she can go away for a holiday or so that she can have a complete rest at home, while knowing that her charge is being well looked after.

Information about financial help Consult the Citizens Advice Bureaux or your nearest reference library for information about aid in your particular area. There are several forms of financial help available, such as attendance allowance, invalid care allowance, mobility allowance or income support. These often vary according to individual income and needs but it is well worth finding out what you are entitled to.

Information about personal help National organisations with local branches, such as Crossroads, provide trained relief carers for short periods only. There is no charge for this service and the majority of their helpers are ex-nurses or people who have worked in caring professions. (For the address, see the end of this book). Write to the Head Office of an appropriate national organisation or contact your local Citizens Advice Bureau or reference library for details of help available in your own area.

Join a group One of the most devastating feelings acknowledged by almost every carer to whom I spoke was the sense of complete isolation – that they were coping alone and unaided with an unending situation. Becoming a member of a group of people in the same sort of position as yourself can give you just the support you need, particularly if you are able to go along to local meetings and share problems and discuss solutions with other people. Even if you are not able to attend the meetings, most support groups have newsletters or telephone crisis lines. Whether you ever need to make use of these or not, it is a relief just to know that they are there.

Make time for yourself It is vital that you find some time to do some of the things that *you* want to do, even if that time has to be snatched when the patient is sleeping or having treatment. Perhaps you can only find the odd fifteen minutes here and there but, when you do, ignore the housework for once, put your feet up and read a magazine or listen to your favourite piece of music.

Case Study: Nora

Although Nora was in a slightly different position, when I first met her she was in a most distressed condition. She was unable to eat or sleep and she was tormented by feelings of guilt. A married woman of sixty-one, she had been caring for her eighty-nine year old mother for several years, even though a mastectomy some ten years earlier had left her with less than excellent health herself. Her mother suffered from progressive senile dementia as well as from many of the physical problems which come with increasing age and decreasing awareness. Nora was the only one around to care for the old lady as her younger brother had emigrated with his family to Canada many years earlier. Her husband had always been supportive and understanding of what Nora saw as her responsibilities but he had now retired and his own health was by no means perfect.

Until very recently her mother had lived just two doors away and Nora had done everything for her. The old lady had taken an irrational dislike to everyone else – the doctor, the district nurse, the succession of home helps – and wanted no one but her daughter to take care of her. She was very difficult to deal with, however, as her condition resulted in frequent confusion and she would become completely unreasonable, berating Nora and scolding her as though she were a disobedient child. Eventually Nora's own physical and mental health deteriorated to such an extent that her doctor became quite concerned and warned her that she was in real danger of a complete breakdown. Gently he pointed out to her that, if this were to happen, there would be no one to care for her mother and the old lady would have to be found a place in a suitable home. He finally succeeded in persuading Nora that it would be better for all concerned if such a place were to be found sooner rather than later while she was still fit and well enough to visit her mother regularly and see that she was being properly looked after.

With the assistance of the local authority, a home was eventually found which had an excellent reputation and which was near enough to her own home for Nora to visit every day. She tried to explain the position to her mother but that lady's mental abilities varied so greatly from day to day that her daughter was never quite sure whether or not she understood. When the day came for her to leave her house and go to the home, however, the old lady had become most distressed and had screamed continuously. Unable to bear the trauma of the situation, Nora had fled to her own home where her husband and her doctor had done their best to comfort her. Ever since that time she had suffered from horrendous nightmares and many other symptoms of stress, even though the move had taken place nearly a year ago. Her mother had now settled down well in the home and was as happy there as she was capable of being. Nora visited her every day – sometimes her mother recognised her and sometimes she did not. This in itself was distressing but, in addition, she felt consumed with guilt for having allowed her to be taken there – and she felt even more guilty because she was conscious of an enormous sense of relief that the day-to-day care of the old lady was now in someone else's hands.

FEELING GUILTY

Guilt is one of the most common emotions among carers. They feel guilty for getting impatient with their charges, or for losing their temper with them. They feel guilty when they believe that they no longer love the person they are caring for, particularly on those occasions when they find themselves wishing that the patient were dead (even though this is usually so that they will no longer suffer rather than for any selfish motive). And yet none of these feelings is uncommon, particularly when the patient is difficult and the carer is approaching the point of exhaustion. However guilt, of course, is one of the greatest causes of stress in any individual.

* *Try not to blame yourself* when you experience feelings which are, after all, completely natural and which are often only temporary and are likely to come to the fore when you are mentally and physically exhausted. You can be sure that you are not alone and that these feelings are common to the majority of other carers too.

* Obviously any final decision – as in Nora's case – must come from you but *do be prepared to take advice from those you trust.* Make lists of the points for and against entrusting the person you have been caring for to professionals. Above all, listen to both your common sense and your own inner feelings. Remember that, although elderly people – particularly those whose minds are no longer clear – hate a break in routine, they will usually settle quite well into a new situation once they are used to it. There is little point in wearing yourself out and causing yourself to be ill if it is to be of no actual benefit to the patient.

* If the decision is made that the person should go into a home – provided you have satisfied yourself that the home is a good one – *try not to waste your energy by permitting too many feelings of guilt.* Use that energy instead to build up your own strength again and to open out your own life in whatever way you wish. Visit your former charge as often as you wish; once you are feeling stronger you will be able to put 100 per cent of yourself into that visit so you will be doing your best for them as well as for yourself.

* Once the worst of the daily burden is lifted from your shoulders, use one or more of the self help techniques given in the next chapter to rebuild your own mental and physical energy.

There is no easy answer to any of the difficulties which arise from being a full time carer. Naturally each case is different and will present different problems. In general, however, it is extremely important to take care of yourself, whether you want to think of this as being a selfish action (for your own well-being) or an unselfish one (so that you will be better able to care for your charge). Make sure that you find out all you can about what you are entitled to, both financially and in the way of moral support. Contact those organisations which can put you in touch with others in a similar position – it really does help to know that you are not alone.

10

Prevention And Cure

I think we would all agree that the amount of stress existing in the second half of the twentieth century is increasing year by year. Nowhere is this stress more acutely felt than by women. After all, in no other section of society have actual lifestyle changes been so dramatic or so rapid. So, what are you going to do about it? How are you going to handle the stress which has already accumulated, whether as a result of a specific problem or simply because of the accumulation of tension brought on by an increasingly frenetic way of life? And, even more important, what steps can you take to ensure that, even if your life is relatively stress-free at the present moment, you are able to remain in control and to avoid the harmful effects of any future stressful situation?

This chapter contains a variety of ways in which you can help to 'de-stress' yourself. I am not suggesting for a moment that you should try and incorporate each and every one of these methods into your daily life – there would be little time left for anything else! But even if you were to concentrate on just one of these ways of self help, you would be bound to notice an improvement. So perhaps you could try several of them, see which ones are best suited to you and fit most conveniently into your daily routine (though possibly you could alter your routine a little if necessary) and just make use of those techniques which most appeal to you.

ALL STRESS IS NOT BAD

Remember that a certain amount of stress in your life will not do you any harm. In fact, in certain circumstances it can be positively beneficial. The extra adrenalin produced when stress is experienced will help you to get out of the way of that oncoming vehicle in the road; that would definitely *not* be an appropriate time for a relaxing breathing exercise! In addition, stress will give you that extra 'oomph' needed to help you think on your feet or come up with innovative ideas just at the right moment. It is only when that stress accumulates without there ever having been an opportunity to reduce its harmful effects that real problems arise.

Know yourself

Make use of the questionnaire in chapter one in order to know and understand yourself and your susceptibility to the harmful effects of stress. You may be surprised at how much you have already been suffering from those effects without even recognising them for what they are.

Perhaps you could also make another list, like the one below:

Things I find stressful	Things I find relaxing

Try and ensure that your life contains elements from each of the two columns - and, if your are unable to find anything to put in the second column, it is vitally important that you set about doing so as soon as possible.

Return to your questionnaire and list from time to time (perhaps every three months or so). In that way you will be able to keep an eye on yourself and (hopefully) note your progress.

Lifestyle changes

Perhaps the easiest way to begin stress-proofing yourself is to try and make some adjustments in your day-to-day lifestyle. These adjustments do not have to be drastic or dramatic but the difference they can make can be significant.

Friends and family   In these days of ever increasing activity it is very easy to become so enmeshed in a daily, weekly or monthly routine that you are more concerned with *doing things* than with *people*. So many women, particularly those who work outside the home, find that they do not seem to have time for their friends any more. Every hour of the working week seems to be spoken for and in the evenings and at weekends they are just too exhausted to bother with visiting or entertaining friends. But friends are vitally important and should be cherished. They provide a part of your life which is nothing to do with work or family – a space where you can be yourself and accepted on your own merits. There is a difference, of course, between friends and acquaintances, but both have a part to play in your life. A real friend will not want to see you only when you are able to provide a lavish meal – a cup of coffee or tea will often do. After all, it is your company which is being sought, not your food. And, if your life really is so hectic that you truly do not have time to see your friends, even for a short time, remember that you can always keep in touch by making that telephone call or writing that letter.

Both the working mother and the one who spends all day caring for a young family may find that there are so many routine tasks to accomplish during the day that conversations with members of the family seem to be limited to 'It's time to get up' or 'Supper's on the table'. And because, in these days of instant entertainment, it is very easy when you are tired simply to flop down in front of the television set or video recorder, communication among the members of many families has all but disappeared.

Talk to your husband/partner/mother/children. Take the time to listen to what they have to say and to understand how they feel. Share yourself and your time with them. One of the best buffers against the stresses of the world is a caring and loving family so try developing the relationships within that unit – you may be surprised to find how much you were missing.

Time for yourself Try and ensure that you are able to set aside a regular time for yourself. It doesn't matter whether we are talking about fifteen minutes each day or a whole afternoon once a week. Everyone needs that 'safety valve', a time when they can please themselves. Perhaps all you will want to do with 'your' time is sit in a chair with your eyes closed and your feet up. Perhaps you would rather pursue some active hobby such as jogging, riding or even hang-gliding! Even if it is simply to indulge in the luxury of a warm bath, knowing that you will not be disturbed, your special time is vitally important – remember, you deserve it.

If you have never before insisted on having some time to yourself, it might be just as well to explain to your partner or family that this does not mean that you are tired of *them* but just that you need a little space in which to re-charge your batteries. (By the way, don't forget to allow *them* some time to themselves too).

Avoid constant competition This applies particularly to those women who work outside the home. It is amazing how many people – men and women – who have to contend all day with the competitive world of business then come home to compete in other ways. Perhaps they play squash or tennis; perhaps their preference is for chess or bridge. All these, and many other pastimes, are competitive by nature and bring with them their own stresses. Now there is no harm at all in indulging in one of these hobbies *provided* you also have some way of spending your time which is definitely non-competitive (even though it may be active) or unless you counteract the effects of stress by following a relaxation routine.

Watch the finances It is natural to want a beautiful home, lovely clothes or splendid holidays and all of these are fine in themselves and can add greatly to your quality of life. The problems arise when the desire for these things exceeds the ability to pay for them or when, in order to have them, you have to stretch yourself to the financial limits. Then stress does indeed creep in; and the harmful effects of that stress can counteract any of the benefits felt.

Do you wait to pay the household bills until you receive final demands and the electricity board is threatening to cut you off? To some people this seems a clever and daring way to live; in other cases either no one has decided who is going to be in charge of dealing with family finances or the chief bill-payer is so absent-minded and forgetful that nothing is done on time. Even if these delaying tactics, whether accidental or deliberate, result in you earning a few pennies in additional interest, I can assure you that the cost in stress will be far greater.

If you are not living alone it is often a good idea to decide who is to be in charge of the payment of household accounts – and preferably to elect the most efficient member of the family! In that way there can be no confusion about who is supposed to do what, and a great deal of stress can be saved.

Make your day longer   Have you ever thought of getting up half an hour earlier or going to bed half an hour later? Before you throw this book out of the window in disgust, stop and think. An extra half hour in the morning can mean a gentler start to the day – and a pleasanter and more relaxed you. As well as giving you time to cope with all those little emergencies which occur in even the most well ordered of lives, an extra thirty minutes in the morning might allow you to have a proper breakfast, a second cup of coffee, to read the newspaper before anyone else gets hold of it, to do the crossword – or just to listen to the birds singing. Try it. Just for a week or two set your alarm to wake you half an hour earlier in the morning. You might feel a bit tired on the first day but, let's face it, getting up is horrible whatever the time! But you might find by the end of the experiment that the extra half an hour is just what you needed to take some of the stress out of your life.

Spread a little tidiness   Nothing could be more uncomfortable than trying to relax in one of those homes which looks as though it comes straight from the coloured pages of one of the more expensive glossy magazines. A home, whether grand or humble, needs to be lived in and enjoyed. But, easy as it is to allow it to accumulate, excessive clutter can be very stressful. Not only is it disturbing in appearance, it often means that you will not be able to find things when you want them.

RELAXATION TECHNIQUES

There are many different relaxation techniques you can learn and practice – and all of them work. What I am going to give you here are two of the most simple and most basic. You can always go on from there to find out about others. Indeed, there are many books on the subject and a number of excellent cassettes on the market to help you.

'I can never relax'. Oh yes, I've heard that one many times. But it just is not true. Relaxation is something which can be learned, just like any other technique. And you are just as capable of learning it as anyone else. You may not feel the benefit after one session, possibly not even after two. But persevere for a couple of weeks and I am sure that you will experience the difference.

What happens when you relax? Just the opposite of what happens when you are suffering from stress:

* your heart rate slows down;
* your blood pressure is reduced;
* the tension in your muscles decreases;
* your output of adrenalin is reduced;
* your body demands less oxygen;
* the flow of blood to organs and muscles is decreased.

All those changes will result in an instant improvement in the way you are feeling. You will feel calmer, more alert, with a greater sense of well being and an increase in energy. And all it takes from you is about fifteen minutes a day practising one of the following exercises:

A basic technique

Perhaps the most basic technique of all – nevertheless it works!

Find a time and place where you can be alone. Shut the door, unplug the telephone, tell everyone you do not wish to be disturbed. You can sit in a chair (though make sure it has a back which is high enough to support your head and neck) or lie on your bed – or even on the floor. Find for yourself the most comfortable position.

Now, close your eyes and tense the muscles in your feet as much as you can and then relax them. Do the same with your legs and your thighs. Then the whole of your body – feel the tension and then the letting go. Now clench your fists and tense your arm muscles and then relax those too. Next comes the part of your body where stress is probably most acutely felt – the area around your head, your neck, your shoulders and your jaw. Tense that part of you – frown and grit your teeth. Then, as you relax those muscles, try and feel the contrast. Let your neck and shoulders relax and then your jaw; let even your eyelids feel heavy.

Spend a few moments breathing slowly and rhythmically. You may find it helpful if you silently count 'one' each time you breathe in and 'two' every time you breathe out.

Once you feel relaxed and comfortable, try and imagine your body growing heavier and heavier – starting with your feet and working up to the top of your head.

Now take your imagination on a walk. You can choose whatever environment most appeals to you. Perhaps you would like to visualise yourself in a country lane or on a sandy beach; then again, you might prefer a shady woodland area or a landscaped garden. This is your image, your place of tranquillity, so make sure that you select surroundings which you really enjoy. Once you have created the picture in your mind, spend a little time getting to know it really well. What can you see around you? What is the weather like? Are there any other people there? Imagine the distant view, the colours, the textures and the scents of the place you have chosen. As you take your imaginary stroll, let your path twist and turn so that there is always something new to see just around the next bend. This will stop you getting bored with the image and 'switching off'.

Some people like to play a piece of gentle music while they relax whereas others prefer total silence. You will have to experiment to see which method suits you best.

Spend ten or fifteen minutes every day practising this exercise and I am sure that you will begin to notice the difference. You may not have changed any of the circumstances around you but your reactions and the amount of stress caused by those circumstances should be very different.

Breathing exercise

The way you breathe and the amount of air you take in affects your looks, your health, your vitality and even your ability to think clearly. And yet very few of us breathe as we really should. With a little practice, however, you can soon learn to improve matters.

The link between stress and breathing is quite easy to see. What happens when you begin to panic? Your breathing becomes shallow and rapid and you are unable to think clearly and rationally. The reverse is also true. If you feel tense or anxious, try making yourself take slow, deep, even breaths and you will not only feel yourself becoming calmer, you will find that you are able to think more clearly and therefore be in control of the situation once more.

There are several excellent breathing exercises but here is one of the basic ones for you to practise. Even if you only find the time to do it for five minutes once or twice a day, you will soon begin to notice the difference. In fact, it is quite a good idea to practise it when you are in bed, just before sleep. Not only will it not take up any of your time during the day but you will probably find that you fall asleep more easily and that the quality of that sleep is vastly improved.

Lie in bed (preferably without pillows until you have completed the exercise). Place your hands on your ribcage so that the tips of your fingers can just touch. Breathe in deeply, making sure that you use your chest and your abdomen. You should be able to feel the expansion of your diaphragm and your fingers should be forced apart. Most people breathe only with the upper part of the body which means that they are not expanding their lungs fully or taking in sufficient oxygen. Without an adequate supply of oxygen, the body is unable to break down the nutrients contained in the food we eat and therefore less energy will be absorbed into the system. When you breathe out you should be able to release just as much air as you previously took in.

If you continue this exercise for about five minutes – twice a day if possible – you will begin to find that you can breathe deeply with your fingertips being forced apart without having to make a determined effort to do so.

SLEEP

We all know and understand the value of a good night's sleep. And yet, when you are stressed, one of the first things you often seem to lose is the ability to sleep soundly. The problems of the day seem to turn over and over in your mind and yet you are unable to come up with any solutions. However tired you are, sleep seems to elude you. In fact the more you try to go to sleep, the more difficult it seems. You know that you need to get some sleep so that you will be fit and well enough to cope with the coming day. You look at the clock and see the hours ticking by and, when you do finally fall asleep, it seems that the alarm sounds just a few moments later, waking you to face another day of growing exhaustion.

Perhaps one of the most misleading phrases in the English language is 'go to sleep'. It causes us to feel that we have actively to *do* something definite to *make* ourselves sleep. Whereas, provided you are able to relax sufficiently, sleep will in fact come to you.

There are many different methods of preparing yourself for sleep, some of which are listed below. Try any or all of them and see if they help you to overcome the problem. But remember, there is no such thing as the 'correct' amount of sleep; we are all different. Just because 'A' needs eight hours a night does not mean that 'B' needs the same. If you are waking refreshed and coping well with your day without suffering from exhaustion, then you are probably having sufficient sleep for your needs.

* There is little point in going to bed while you still feel bright and alert. Do something which gives you pleasure – read a book, listen to some music – rather than trying to fit in that extra piece of work.

* Think about your eating habits. Certain vitamin and mineral deficiencies can lead to sleeping difficulties.

* A stuffy atmosphere makes sleeping much more difficult. Try to ensure that neither you nor anyone else smokes in the bedroom as, even if you manage to get to sleep, you are likely to wake with a 'fuzzy' head.

* Ensure that you have time for some sort of physical exercise during the course of each day. It does not have to be a regimented routine – a walk around the block would do – and, if you are someone who normally has difficulty sleeping, naturally you won't take this exercise just before retiring for the night.

* Avoid drinking stimulating drinks, such as tea and coffee, too late in the evening. The caffeine they contain could well keep you awake.

* Alcohol too should be avoided late in the evening. You might feel tempted to have a 'nightcap' but, even though late night alcohol might help you to fall asleep quickly, you are far more likely to have a disturbed night, possibly waking several times.

* There are some drinks which are sleep-inducing. If you do not have a health condition which precludes it, there is much to be said for a cup of warm milk just before bedtime. Health shops now sell tea bags of herbal mixtures which are said to help you to sleep. You could try one of these or simply stick to good old fashioned chamomile tea. (Its taste is vastly improved if you add a teaspoonful of honey to it).

* Just as you can develop a routine of not sleeping, you can establish a pre-bedtime routine which will help to prepare you mentally for sleep. There is a great deal to be said for doing the same things just before bed each night as your subconscious mind will automatically form a liaison between those actions and the sleep which is to follow. So feed the cat, draw the curtains, put out the milk bottles, wash your tights – it doesn't matter what you do provided you establish a nightly routine.

* If you like to have a bath just before going to bed, take care over the temperature of the water. A bath which is either too hot or too cold will simply act as a stimulant.

* Once you are in bed, practise either the relaxation exercise or the breathing exercise already given and remember that you are far more likely to sleep deeply and well if you give up the idea of 'going' to sleep. Just relax and let it come to you.

EATING HABITS

Anyone whose diet is basically healthy and provides all the necessary vitamins and minerals is far more able to cope with the physical effects of stress. And at least this is an area where you are the one in control. *You* are the person who decides what you eat and drink.

I am not advocating an impossibly strict regime of dietary rules and health foods. Any form of fanaticism is harmful and you might well increase the amount of stress you experience if you allow yourself to feel deprived of your favourite foods. All I am suggesting is that you try to ensure that your diet is as balanced and healthy as possible and, if there is any particular range of foods which you find unpalatable, that you consider supplementing your diet with any of the reputable brands of vitamin and mineral tablets.

How do you know whether or not you are suffering from a vitamin or mineral deficiency? It is not easy to tell but study the list below and, if you find that any of the symptoms apply to you, it may be worth while checking more closely the content of what you are eating.

The most common symptoms of vitamin and mineral deficiency are:

* dry, flaking skin;
* a very red tongue;
* white flecks or ridges on your fingernails;
* frequent occurrences of bleeding gums or mouth ulcers;
* dull, lifeless hair;
* dry skin at the corners of your mouth and around your nose;
* a tendency to bruise easily;
* slow healing from cuts or grazes;
* a low energy level.

If you feel that you are deficient in any of the essential vitamins or minerals, it may be that all you need to do is make some simple changes to your eating habits or to take a multivitamin tablet each day. And at least here is one area of your life where the cure lies in your own hands.

EXERCISE

No, I am not suggesting that you have to sweat it out at a gymnasium five nights a week. Nor do I wish to conjure up painful recollections of school PE lessons. Exercise does not have to be an unpleasant and harrowing experience. There are so many ways in which you can fit some form of exercise into your daily life that you are bound to find one which suits you.

You may be wondering why you should bother with any formal type of exercise at all. After all, you lead an active life, always rushing from one place to another, hardly ever having time to sit down. Isn't that exercise enough? The answer, I'm afraid, is no. Not only are you not doing yourself any real good with all that frenetic activity, the stress brought about by the constant rushing around could actually be doing you harm.

Physical fitness of the sort created by making regular exercise part of your weekly routine is a great protection against stress-related illness. The muscles around your heart become stronger, your breathing is more efficient and therefore more beneficial, your circulation improves – and you feel better in yourself.

Exercise does not have to take you crashing through the pain barrier in order to be effective. In fact, the best form of exercise is one which is both regular and controlled. You may find that, while the thought of jogging fills you with horror, you quite enjoy a trip to the local leisure centre for a swim. It may be that you do not enjoy any sports activity at all but that you are quite happy to exercise for twenty minutes or so at home and on your own, perhaps while listening to your favourite music. The choice is yours but whatever form of exercise you choose, bear the following points in mind.

* If you have a fairly competitive lifestyle, try and choose a form of exercise which is not competitive too. The stress brought on by the element of competition could well nullify the benefits of the exercise itself.

* Exercise should be regular to be effective. If you do little more than walk from your front door to the car for six days a week and then attempt the marathon at the weekend, you are far more likely to do yourself harm than good. The ideal minimum is approximately twenty minutes of sustained exercise three times a week.

* Choose something you enjoy! If you decide to attend an aerobics class, even though you hate it, because you think it will do you good, you will never keep it up. Perhaps all you want to do is have a good brisk walk three times a week and that is fine – provided you ensure that it *is* brisk.

* Start slowly. If you have not been exercising recently, it would not do you any good at all to throw yourself into a routine which leaves you feeling mentally and physically exhausted. Of course, if you think or know that you are not very fit, or

if you are aware of a chronic medical condition, you would be wise to take advice before embarking on a programme of physical exercise. You should be able to hold a normal conversation after a period of exercise and, if you cannot do so, perhaps you are over-doing things and should proceed more slowly.

MEDITATION

What does the word 'meditation' mean to you? To many people it conjures up an image of open-toed sandals, joss-sticks and an omnipotent guru with strange robes and a shaven head. But nothing could be further from the truth. Meditation is a method of discovering an inner peace and does not have to affect your own philosophy or your religious beliefs in any way.

If you wish you can study meditation under the guidance of an experienced teacher or within a group. But it is also possible to learn meditation quite successfully on your own and in your own home. Unless you are seeking to impose impossibly high standards upon yourself, the only commitment you need to make is ten or fifteen minutes a day of your time.

There is a difference between relaxation and meditation. When you practise relaxation, your attention is focused on yourself – on the release of muscular tension or the rhythm of your breathing. This can be extended to become a form of meditation in itself. With other methods of meditation, however, you learn to focus your attention on an external object (which can be real or imaginary). This object can be a word, an image, a sound or a concept. The following is a simple meditation exercise for you to try: Depending on how supple you are, you can either sit cross-legged on the floor or kneel back on your heels, or else sit on a firm, straight-backed chair with your feet flat on the floor. The important thing is that you should be able to remain comfortable for ten to fifteen minutes without slumping. Rest your hands in your lap, gently close your eyes and allow your breathing to settle into a quiet rhythm. After a minute or two silently begin to repeat the single word 'peace' each time you breathe out. Remember this is *not* a deep breathing exercise – simply use your gentle out-breath to help focus your attention on the word 'peace'. Continue for ten minutes – or as long as you feel comfortable – and then slowly open your eyes, stretch, smile and go about your business.

The benefits of meditation are many and, although you will not be aware of them from the first day, nonetheless it takes less time than you would imagine to experience them. Some of the recognised benefits are:

* slowing down of heart/pulse rate;
* lowering of blood pressure;
* improvement in circulation;
* improvement in breathing;
* dramatic reduction in level of stress experienced;
* improvement in amount and quality of sleep;
* improvement in concentration;
* increase of awareness;
* reduction in addiction (to food, alcohol, tobacco, drugs);
* improvement in memory;
* increased sense of well being.

OTHER FORMS OF HELP

There are various forms of outside help of which you can avail yourself in your effort to overcome or prevent a build-up of stress. Never feel that you are a failure as an individual if you need to consult an expert – after all, you do not think you have failed when your tooth aches and you visit a dental surgeon, do you? It may be that you are one of those people who prefer to seek professional assistance or it may be that you prefer to do everything for yourself. The choice is yours. As long as the end result is that you are free from the negative effects of excessive stress, it really does not matter.

As well as various helpful books and tapes which are on the market (some of which are listed at the end of this book), there are experts in various fields whom you can consult:

Massage

While therapeutic massage is an excellent way of inducing physical and mental relaxation in everyone, it is of particular benefit to those people who spend a large part of their day sitting at a desk or in front of a computer screen. Massage or manipulation reduces the muscle tension which encourages extreme activity in the central nervous system. This in turn prevents you 'switching off' at the end of the day and can lead to restless and disturbed nights.

In addition to releasing muscular tension, massage stimulates the flow of blood within the body and this brings a sense of relaxation to your body and tranquillity to your mind.

Shiatsu

This is a form of healing which originated in Japan and it should only ever be carried out by a skilled practitioner as it requires pressure on acupuncture points.

Aromatherapy

Aromatherapy is physical massage with the use of specially blended essential oils. The oils are made from natural sources and are combined with a neutral base. Different oils are used to help counteract various problems relating to the mind or the body and a qualified aromatherapist will usually spend some time working on a detailed diagnosis of you as an individual before deciding which oil – or combination of oils – to use.

Alexander Technique

By teaching you to use your body correctly, the Alexander Technique (so named because it was devised by an actor, F.M. Alexander) is able to correct many physiological conditions. It is not merely something to practise when you feel most tense – it is a way of life. By learning how to use your body correctly at all times, physical tension is never allowed to accumulate. This, of course, is a great help in freeing yourself of both mental and emotional stress too. Instruction in the Alexander Technique should always be given by a professionally qualified teacher.

Hypnotherapy

Hypnosis is not used simply to help you to stop smoking or lose weight. In fact, as a hypnotherapist myself, I can assure you that about 75 per cent of my patients consult me because of a stress-related problem. Perhaps they cannot sleep, they experience anxiety attacks or they suffer from migraine or phobias. The list of stress-related conditions is endless.

The essential first stage of hypnosis is the bringing about of a feeling of deep relaxation – and that, in itself, can be extremely beneficial. In fact, many patients tell me that this first stage alone has helped them to overcome what they had hitherto considered to be chronic conditions.

Many people are dissuaded from consulting a hypnotherapist because of the 'Svengali-image' so beloved by film makers and, sadly, reinforced by certain stage and television hypnotists. In fact, it is the patient who is in full charge of the situation at all times. Nothing will happen which he or she does not wish to happen. If you consult a hypnotherapist, you will always hear and understand everything which is taking place and, should you decide that you do not wish to proceed, all you have to do is open your eyes – and it is all over. At no time will you be out of control in any way at all. The task of the hypnotherapist is not to *do* anything to you but simply to help you to help yourself in whichever way you choose.

Yoga

No, you do not have to stand on your head nor yet to contort your body into unbelievable knots. Of course some advanced practitioners of yoga may well be able to perform such feats but the basic yoga technique is designed to enable any of us to balance mind, body and spirit and to experience the calmness and serenity such balance naturally induces. Imbalance creates tension and internal conflict. Yoga works to resolve this conflict and restore inner peace.

Classes in yoga are now widely available and, in addition, there are some excellent cassettes on the subject. These are often graded according to the ability and experience of the pupil and, provided you choose a reputable one (which will normally include a diagram of correct positions) they are quite suitable for home use.

THE POWER OF THE MIND

You may have done all that you can to prevent or eliminate the effects of stress by correcting your eating habits, practising relaxation, taking sufficient exercise and so on. But what can you do about those areas over which you have no control – the outside influences which cause you to suffer a great deal of stress and tension? You can use your mind and your imagination to help you.

Anxious anticipation is probably the cause of more mental stress than anything else. And, although we know that a limited amount of stress can be good for you, what can you do when the tension caused by the anticipation of coming events seems to overwhelm you? Try asking yourself a few questions:

* *What am I frightened of?* Putting your fears into words can also put them into perspective. Whether you speak your thoughts to a sympathetic listener or whether you simply write them down on a piece of paper, it will help you to see the situation clearly.

* *What is the worst that can happen?* Suppose all your anxieties prove to be correct – what is the worst that can happen to you? You are unlikely to lose your life or every possession you own. Analyse the situation, consider the very worst outcome and how you would deal with it. After that, anything else has to be an improvement and easier to handle.

* *What is fear about the future doing to my present?* Naturally we all have to think about the future and make plans as far as we are able. But do you spend so much time worrying about what is going to happen tomorrow that you forget to enjoy any of today? Once you have asked yourself what it is that you are frightened of and once you have decided how you would deal with the worst outcome you can imagine, put the matter to one side if you can. Otherwise you may find yourself spending your entire life worrying about things which never happen and suddenly the days, weeks, months and years will have passed without you ever having stopped to enjoy any of them.

BEING PREPARED

There is a great deal to be said in favour of being prepared, particularly if the event for which you are preparing yourself is one which has been causing you anxiety. In just the same way that an actor will rehearse his part in order to give as perfect a performance as possible, you can mentally rehearse any situation so that you are able to cope with it when it arises. From driving tests to interviews; from examinations to presentations; a great deal of the tension can be erased from any situation where you would normally expect to suffer from 'nerves'. Provided you have sufficient notice of the coming event, give yourself several days, if not a couple of weeks, in which to indulge in mental rehearsal. Then, having found a quiet time and place where you are able to relax, play through the anticipated scene in your imagination, seeing everything in your mind just as you would like it to turn out in reality. Then, when you find yourself faced with the actual situation, it will be far less daunting as you will have done it all before. Anything is less frightening once it has been done before, even if only in your mind.

* * *

If you know that you suffer from stress, then any or all of the methods given in this chapter will help to alleviate the situation. If you do not feel that you are stressed, try them anyway. It will certainly mean that you are far more able to cope with any stressful situation when it arises and, if you start to feel a real improvement in your physical and mental state, it may be that you were more subject to the effects of stress than you thought.

Useful Information

ORGANISATIONS

Tranquillizer addiction

Tranx,
25a Masons Avenue
Wealdstone, Harrow,
Middx.

MIND
22 Harley Street
London W1N 2ED

Safety when driving

Mobile Security Courses
Driving Management Ltd.
Audubon House
Bradcutts Lane
Cookham, Berks. SL6 9AA

Imitation car phones from:
Topical House
15 Frogmore Rd.
Apsley, Hemel Hempstead
Herts. HP3 9RW

Going back to work

Working Mothers' Association
77 Holloway Road
London N7 8JZ

Women Returners Network
Chelmsford Adult Education
   Centre
Patching Hall Lane
Chelmsford, Essex CM1 4DB

The Pepperell Unit
The Industrial Society
Robert Hyde House
48 Bryanston Square
London W1H 7LN

National Childminder's
   Association
8 Masons Hill
Bromley
Kent
BR2 9EY

Useful information

Dealing with bereavement

Cruse
Cruse House
126 Sheen Road
Richmond, Surrey TW9 1UR

Compassionate Friends
6 Denmark Street
Bristol BS1 5DQ

Help for Carers

Crossroads Care Attendant
  Scheme
10 Regent Place
Rugby, Warks. CV21 2PV

Association of Carers
Medway Homes
Balfour Road
Rochester, Kent ME4 6QU

Stress Management
  Workshops

Laura Vale
The Hypnothink Foundation
PO Box 154
Cheltenham, Glos. GL54 9EG

Alexander Technique

Society of Teachers of the
Alexander Technique
10 London House
266 Fulham Road
London SW10 9EL

Hypnotherapy

The Hypnothink Foundation
PO Box 154
Cheltenham, Glos. GL53 9EG

Yoga

British Wheel of Yoga
1 Hamilton Place
Boston Road
Sleaford
Lincs. NG34 7ES

Yoga for Health Foundation
Ickwell Bury
Northill
Biggleswade
Beds. SG18 9BR

British School of Yoga
24 Osney Crescent
Paignton, Devon TQ4 5EY

Meditation

Transcendental Meditation
Baker Street Centre
24 Linhope Street
London NW1

Sivananda Yoga Vedanta
  Centre
50 Chapstow Villas
London W11 2QY

Siddha Meditation
Campenton, Riverside
Temple Gardens
Staines, Middx. TW18 3NS

Further Reading

Managing Stress by Ursula Markham (Element Books, 1989)
Stress and Relaxation by Leslie Kenton (Century Hutchinson 1986)
Fit for Life by Donald Norfolk (Hamlyn, 1980)
Holistic Living by Patrick Pietroni (Dent, 1986)
A Death in the Family by Marion Wright (Macdonald Optima, 1987)
How to Stand Up for Yourself by Dr. Paul Hauck (Sheldon Press 1981)
Life Without Tranquillizers by Vernon Coleman (Piatkus, 1987)
Women and Fatigue by Holly Atkinson (Macmillan 1987)
Hypnothink by Ursula Markham (Thorsons, 1985)

CASSETTES ON RELAXATION AND SELF HELP

Available from:

Thorsons Publishing Group Ltd.,
Denington Estate
Wellingborough
Northants NN8 2RQ

The Hypnothink Foundation
PO Box 154
Cheltenham, Glos. GL53 9EG

INDEX